Everything About Guitar Scales

BY WILBUR M. SAVIDGE

Exclusive Publication Rights:
PRAXIS MUSIC PUBLICATIONS, INC.

Credits:

Graphic Design — Cover .... John McDearmon
Technical Supervision .... Randy L. Vradenburg
Production Manager .... W.M. Savidge
Proof Reading .... Ken Nance
Typesetting .... Team Graphix, Inc.
Typesetting — Music Notation .... W.R. Music Service
Printing/Color Separations ..... European Color Scan, Inc.

Cover Guitar:
Gibson Les Paul "Standard"
Courtesy — C&S Music, Fort Worth

A PRODUCT OF PRAXIS MUSIC PUBLICATIONS, INC.
Bedford, Texas

A

A PERSONAL OBSERVATION

All human endeavor great or small does, it seems, evolve from learning experiences. Certainly learning to play the guitar, however well, requires many hours of practice. Not everyone who takes up the instrument has the "stick-to-it-iveness" required. In my many years of teaching, I have tried to identify those qualities a student must possess in order to succeed. Desire, patience, talent and personal study habits are key factors. However, I found one quality that all successful people, musicians included, have in abundance. I first observed this a number of years ago in an individual who never played the guitar, or any instrument. This young man, in fact, did not enjoy the physical abilities or intellectual skills possessed by most people. Yet, this one characteristic allowed him to overcome his physical disabilities and make many seemingly impossible accomplishments in his short lifetime.

What he possessed and used to its fullest in everything he attempted was the gift of "persistence". The inborn willingness to stick to the job at hand, no matter how difficult it seemed. Through persistence, he overcame his limitations and showed all who knew him what could be accomplished if a person really wanted something badly enough. It is with this thought in mind that I dedicate this book in memory of:

"Jonathan Martin Savidge"

Bill Savidge

SCALES, SCALES, SCALES . . .

Scales are the building blocks of music — melody, chords and harmony. Competent musicians understand and are able to play scales fluently. Regardless of specialization of instrument, knowledge of scales allows freedom of expression and the capability to "create". Early-on in the study of scales from material in this book and other sources, you begin to realize how complicated and physically demanding this study may become. How many ways (patterns) of playing the C Major scale do you, as a guitarist, want to know? How many scale forms will be adequate to express your own musical ideas?

There are many fingerings, patterns and positions for playing any scale. Some are fairly easy to play, others are complex and difficult. Is the technical skill required to play scales in all positions on the fingerboard worth the study effort? This of course, only you can determine.

The scale forms presented in this book are, by necessity, limited. It is possible to "create" new, more complex scale patterns daily — a time-consuming study of the guitar fingerboard. The scale positions presented within the scope of this text provide a sound foundation in scale forms, technical skill and general understanding of scale usage. This information will improve your playing and provide you with the "tools" to compose and play melodies in any key.

"EVERYTHING ABOUT GUITAR SCALES", is the name of this book. "Everything", is a vast, complicated subject! The information herein has been designed to be *practical* information. In order to know "everything" about the subject of scales, purchase every book on the subject you come across. All authors approach the subject from a different perspective. You *can* gain new information from every book you study.

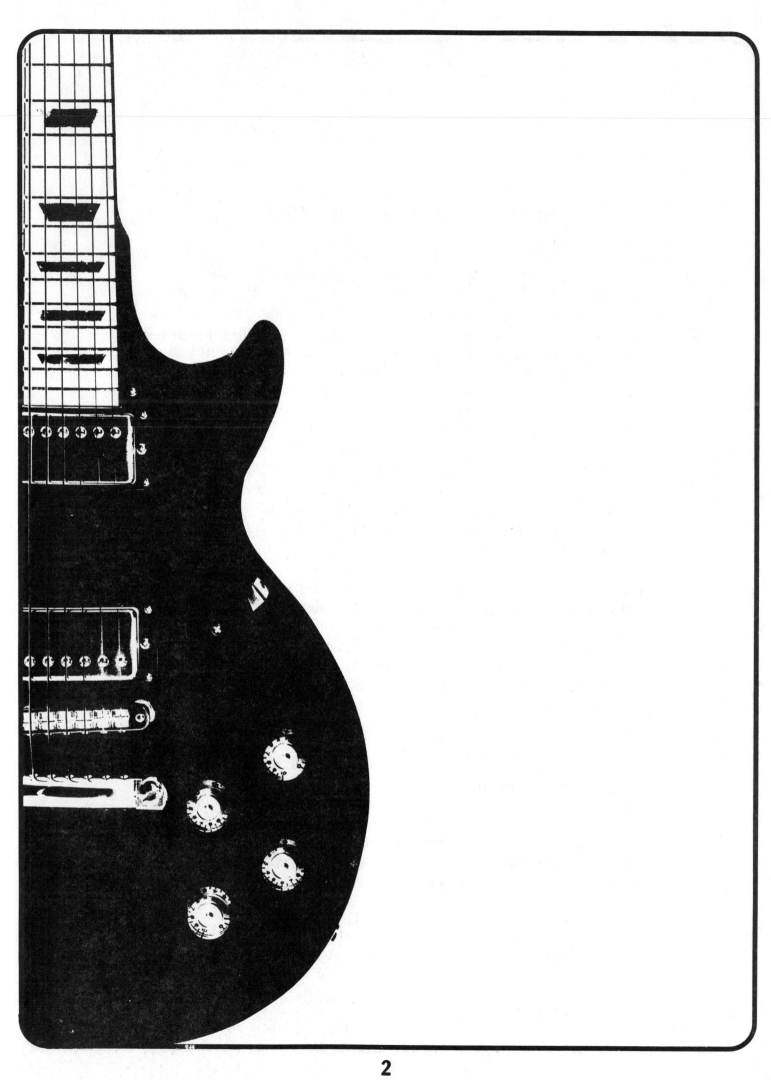

TABLE OF CONTENTS

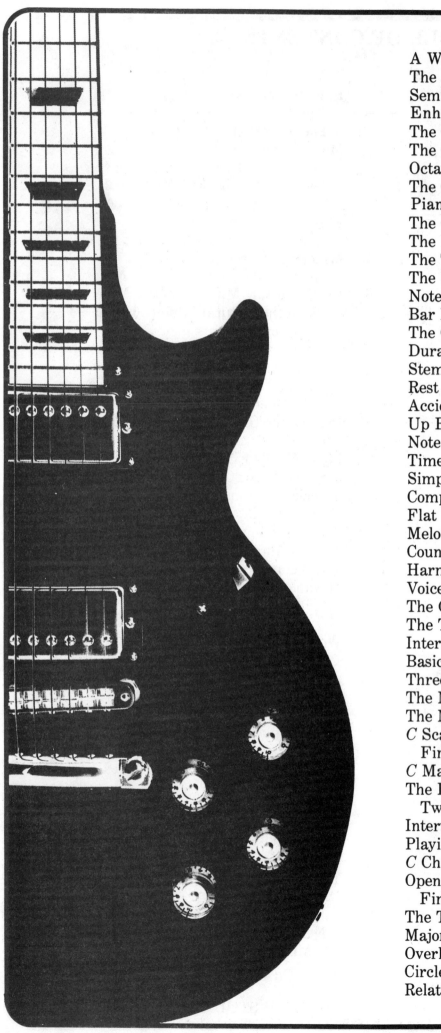

ELEMENTS OF MUSIC

ELEMENTS of MUSIC
ELEMENTS of MUSIC
ELEMENTS of MUSIC
ELEMENTS of MUSIC
ELEMENTS of MUSIC
ELEMENTS of MUSIC
ELEMENTS of MUSIC
ELEMENTS of MUSIC
ELEMENTS of MUSIC
ELEMENTS of MUSIC
ELEMENTS of MUSIC
ELEMENTS of MUSIC
ELEMENTS of MUSIC
ELEMENTS of MUSIC
ELEMENTS of MUSIC
ELEMENTS of MUSIC
ELEMENTS of MUSIC
ELEMENTS of MUSIC

THE ELEMENTS OF MUSIC

What is your impression of a piece of sheet music? If you know absolutely nothing about music, you probably see a mass of black dots and circles and a few other mysterious signs scattered about on a regularly arranged series of five lines. However, if you look closely at a written arrangement (*Illustration One*), even the most unmusical amateur will perceive that there is a certain symmetry, an apparent order and logic about the way everything is arranged. A page of written music provides clear, precise, instruction enabling the musician, amateur or professional to correctly create on their instrument the musical tonalities written by the song arrangers.

Not all sounds are music. The sounds best used for musical creation are well defined, clear and pleasant, with the combining of tones in such melodic, harmonic and rhythmic progression (movement) as to provide an agreeable and intelligible effect. They can be produced on the guitar by causing the strings to vibrate, either by plucking the strings with our fingers, or by striking the strings with a pick (plectrum).

Properly tuned, the guitar will produce pleasant musical tones that will vary in PITCH (high or low in the scale), intensity and duration. High notes are the sounds of fast vibrations set in motion by the smaller high pitch guitar strings; low notes are the sounds of slow vibrations as produced by the larger bass strings on the guitar.

All music is based on the proven scientific fact that notes we use in a musical SCALE have fixed rates of vibration which are mathematically related to one another. A musician learns how to produce the proper notes on his instrument. The song's composer tells the musician what notes to play. Written music is the musician's guide. How do we interpret this information? This is the secret that we must discover before we can understand music and play written arrangements on the guitar.

THE MUSICAL ALPHABET

The black and white piano keyboard (*Illustration Two*) presents music theory in a visual pattern not so obvious on a stringed instrument like the guitar. The recurring pattern of black and white keys help the musician to find the notes easily. Each note in music is represented by a corresponding key. Each piano key is the name of a musical note. The musical alphabet consists of seven letters: A B C D E F G, (the white keys, continuously repeat from the left end of the keyboard). If you move from any note to the one next to it, a white or black key on the piano (*Illustration Three*), you will have moved through a HALF TONE, also called a SEMI-TONE or HALF-STEP. If you move upwards a semi-tone, you have played a SHARP (written as #). If you move a semi-tone descending in pitch, you will have played a FLAT (written b). The black and white keys are arranged in a repetitive pattern of black and white keys. The black keys place a SHARP or FLAT called ACCIDENTALS between a pattern of white keys.

ENHARMONIC CHANGE

An ACCIDENTAL, sharp or flat is named in relation to its closest white note on the piano keyboard, (*Illustration Four*). The note produced by the black key, spaced between A and B, for example, may be called either A#, meaning a sharp or RAISED A; or Bb, meaning a flat or LOWERED B. Unless the key signature specifies otherwise, a note is called a sharp when ascending and a flat when descending.

The piano keyboard consists of the following groups of keys: The white keys A B C D E F G, and the black keys or accidentals, sharps A# C# D# F# G#, or the flats Ab Bb Db Eb Gb.

THE MUSICAL ALPHABET

ILLUSTRATION ONE
A WRITTEN ARRANGEMENT

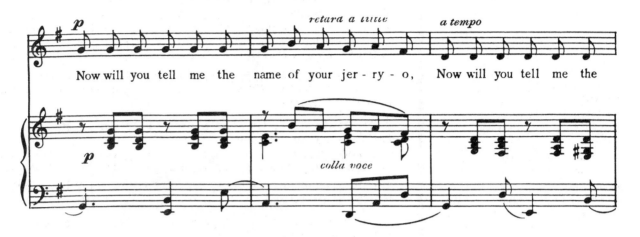

ILLUSTRATION TWO
THE PIANO KEYBOARD

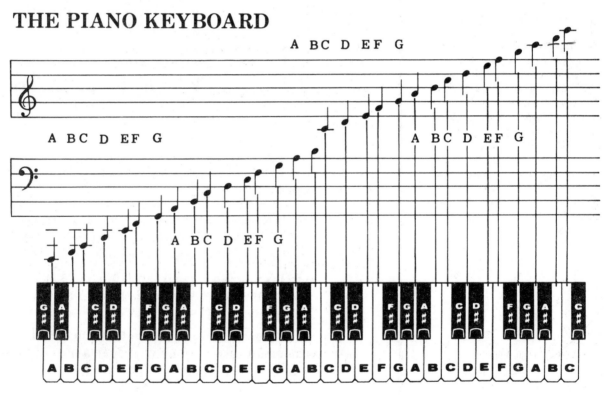

ILLUSTRATION THREE
SEMI-TONE/HALF-TONE

ILLUSTRATION FOUR
ENHARMONIC CHANGE

The Greeks created and experimented with a scale comprised of twelve half-tones known as the Chromatic Scale. In the late Renaissance there were attemps to revive these smaller tonal intervals. This new music exhibited a degree of chromaticism, which provided a greater feeling of tension in the melodic line and greater freedom of melodic expression. These new tones were called Accidentals, simply because they were not natural to the musical scales previously in use. Additional Signs were then introduced to represent accidentals, our symbols for the Sharp and Flat (# b).

CHROMATIC SCALE

The seven white keys, *A B C D E F G*, and the five black keys spaced between the white keys represent the twelve notes of the musical alphabet. These notes, played in succession, ascending or descending in pitch through twelve half-steps is called a CHROMATIC SCALE (*Illustration One*). When the original note name repeats the thirteenth tone, we have played an OCTAVE. The octave note repeats the original, doubling frequency (*A* to *A*, *B* to *B*, etc.). The piano keyboard is a twelve tone chromatic scale repeating in octaves.

THE OCTAVE

Whenever TWO notes of the same name, but one of different pitch, one written higher than the other and vice versa, they are said to be an OCTAVE apart. An octave occurs when the pitch sequence is placed thirteen notes above or below the first note. Two notes an octave apart will sound the same, but will have different pitches; one will be in a higher range or REGISTER than the other. This is a natural phenomenon of sound. It is important to realize that an octave does not consist of thirteen notes, but is the thirteenth note above the first of a series of twelve successive notes.

THE CHROMATIC SCALE

ILLUSTRATION ONE

THE CHROMATIC SCALE

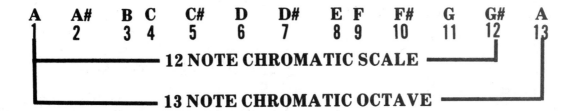

ILLUSTRATION TWO

12 CHROMATIC SCALES

A A# B C C# D D# E F F# G G# A
  A# B C C# D D# E F F# G G# A A#
    B C C# D D# E F F# G G# A A# B
      C C# D D# E F F# G G# A A# B C
        C# D D# E F F# G G# A A# B C C#
          D D# E F F# G G# A A# B C C# D
            D# E F F# G G# A A# B C C# D D#
              E F # G G# A A# B C C# D D# E
                F F# G G# A A# B C C# D D# E F
                  F# G G# A A# B C C# D D# E F F#
                    G G# A A# B C C# D D# E F F# G
                      G# A A# B C C# D D# E F F# G G#

ILLUSTRATION THREE

THE CHROMATIC SCALE IN WRITTEN FORM

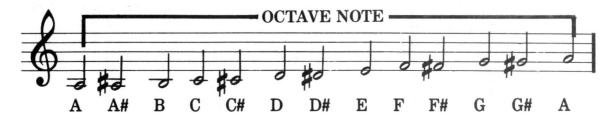

9

During the thirteenth century, two instruments evolved from the lute family — the Guitarra Morica, *and* Guitarra Latina. *The guitarra morica had a pronounced arched back and in the fifteenth century became the* Mandola, *an instrument with four double strings, the forerunner of our modern mandolin.*

The guitarra latina, with its flat back and oval belly curving to a point at the top led to the development, in the thirteenth century, of the Viheula, *an instrument with a flat sound-box, short backward bent neck, and a peg box mounted at an angle.*

During the Classical period, the curvature of the sound-box became more pronounced and the guitar was strung with double courses (pairs of strings), a Spanish influence. At this time, the French and Italians used single courses which were easier to tune, and in time, they came to be the standard string set for later guitars.

The early sixteenth century guitar had four gut strings. In the second half of the century, the fifth and sixth strings appeared, expanding the instrument tonal range.

Because of the Spanish influence in guitar design, the pinched waist, sound-hole design and placement, and written compositions for the Guitarra Esponolo — *the guitar became known as the* Spanish Guitar.

FRETS

The early fourteenth century lute was a stepped, chromatic instrument. The neck was divided into semi-tones by thin gut ligaments, tied and knotted around it which came to be called Frets.

Gut frets worked well. However, they quickly became loose, moved and no longer occupied the correct place on the neck required to create the exact pitch of each note. Proper intonation of the instrument was a near impossibility.

THE COMPLETE GUITAR FINGERBOARD

The division of the chromatic scale into twelve half-steps (semi-tones), is accomplished on the guitar fingerboard by the placement of the fingerboard frets.

The six strings of the guitar make up six CHROMATIC SCALES. Each chromatic scale starts on the note in the scale upon which the guitar string is tuned. On the guitar, the chromatic scale starts with the open (unfretted) string, and continues up the neck, ascending in pitch until we repeat the open tone again at the twelfth fret. Twelve frets, each corresponding to one key on the piano, plus the open string note, equals thirteen notes or one complete octave.

THE GUITAR FINGERBOARD

THE
COMPLETE
GUITAR FINGER BOARD

(12 FRETS PLUS THE OPEN STRINGS)

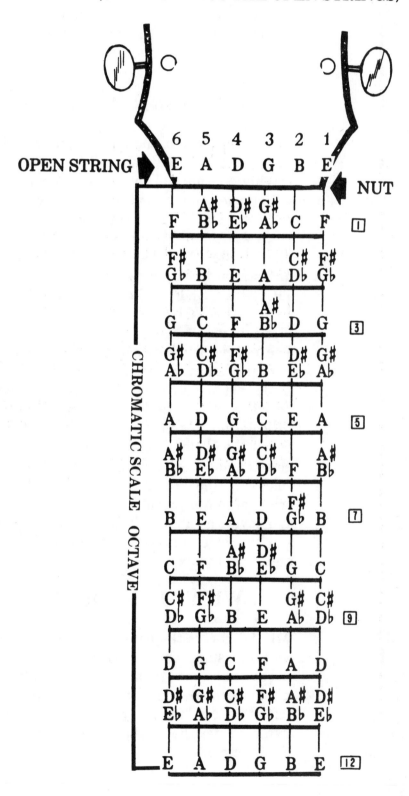

ELEMENTS OF MUSIC

In 1709, an instrument maker from Florence, Italy, Bartolommeo Cristofori, introduced a new instrument, a further development of the harpsichord. The special construction of this instrument allowed the performer to vary the volume and tone simply by how hard the keys were struck. This revolutionary development, which Cristofori called a "gravicembalo col piano e forte", roughly translated means: a gravity-operated harpsichord with loudness and softness. This opened up a new realm of musical expression, and our modern dynamic expression of nuances became possible. With further technical development, the name of the instrument was shortened to "piano-forte", and finally to "piano".

In the tenth century, Italian writers developed a line, called a "staff", that signified a certain main note in the middle register of a melody. Then higher sounds would be written above it, and the lower sounds underneath. This allowed the melody to be seen. This was the beginning of "diastemic notation" (from the Greek "diastema", or interval).

In time as this simplified system improved, a second line was added at the interval of a fifth, then a fourth line, each drawn in different colors. Each line was marked at the beginning with a letter corresponding to the note it represented. From these letters, the clef signs were derived and colored lines were no longer used. The modern treble clef 𝄞 evolved from the letter G drawn in medieval graphic writing. The placement of the treble clef at the beginning of the staff means that the second line of the staff is G above middle C, and is performed by the higher pitched instruments or voices. The placement of the bass clef 𝄢 before a staff means that the fourth line up is usually played by the lower pitched instruments or voices.

PIANO-FORTE STAVE (Staff)

Keyboard music was originally written on an eleven line, ten space staff called the GREAT STAVE (staves is the plural of staff) (*Illustration One*), a device created during the Middle Ages for the written notation of organ music. This was confusing and did not differentiate between those notes played by the left hand and those played by the right hand.

THE MODERN PIANO STAFF

In classical usage, the middle line was dropped out of the Great Stave (*Illustration Two*), leaving the note *C* suspended in mid-space, with the left hand playing the notes written on the lower staff and the right hand playing the notes written on the upper staff. This is commonly called PIANO-FORTE music: two five line staffs, the upper staff identified by the TREBLE CLEF &, the lower staff identified by the BASS CLEF .

The distinction between the treble clef and bass clef is important. The notes *A B C D E F G* do not occupy the same position on or between the staff lines in each case (*Illustration Three*). The treble clef is also called the *G* clef, because it encompasses the note *G* and covers a range suitable for higher voices and the pitch of the guitar. The bass clef or *F* clef centers around the *F* below Middle *C*, and covers a range suitable for the low voices and the lower pitched instruments (the bass guitar and viola).

WHAT IS MIDDLE C?

MIDDLE *C* is the note separating the treble and bass staffs on a piano score. It is the tone produced by the *C* nearest to the middle of the piano keyboard (the white key immediately left of the two black keys nearest to the piano name above the keyboard on a traditional acoustic piano).

THE STAFF

THE PIANO-FORTE STAVE (STAFF)

ILLUSTRATION ONE

THE GREAT STAVE

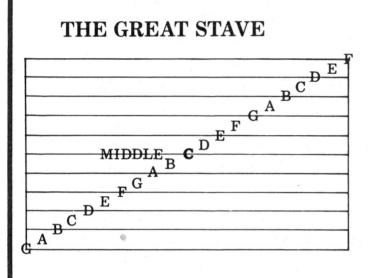

ILLUSTRATION TWO

PIANO-FORTE

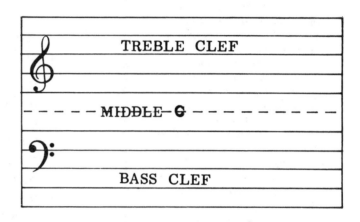

ILLUSTRATION THREE

THE MODERN PIANO STAFF

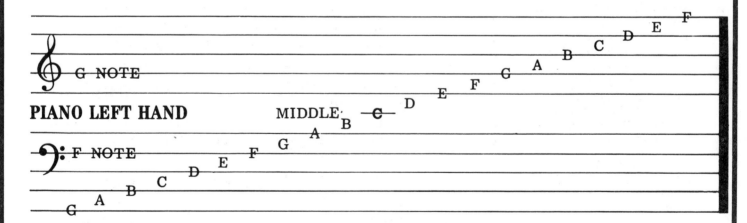

ELEMENTS OF MUSIC

The development of the modern musical staff is credited to a Benedictine monk by the name of Guido of Arezzo (995-1050). Guido established the predecessor of our modern diatonic scale, a six-tone scale called the "hexachord", using the CDEFGA pattern. He also established a precise level of pitch for each note associating each note of the scale with a Latin syllable, thereby creating the familiar pattern of syllables used to this day. This enables singers to know how each note of the scale should sound in relationship to all other notes of the scale —the "do re fa sol la ti", system.

Guido's musical staff was a group of four horizontal lines that represented different tones, upon which one could record precisely a series of notes and their specific pitch in relationship to a series of notes. Guido's staff of four lines and three spaces contained the full range of notes in the hexachord. If a melody contained a broad range of low and higher tones that spanned more than one hexachord, it was necessary to establish a common point of reference. This was achieved by the designation of "middle C", and the use of the treble and bass clef symbols.

THE STAFF

Notes placed on any of the lines, or spaces between, are given specific names indicating PITCH. The individual lines and spaces are also numbered for reference *(Illustration One)*. The lines *(Illustration Two)* are named: *E G B D F*, and may be easily memorized by the sentence *Every Good Boy Does Fine*. The spaces *(Illustration Three)* are named: *F A C E*, and spell the word "face".

LEDGER LINES

The five line staff does not provide room to write many notes, certainly the tonal range of the piano and guitar, as well as many other instruments, extend below and above the staff.

Should we wish to write notes above or below the staff, we must extend the staff lines. These lines are called LEDGER LINES *(Illustration Four)*, and are written in an abbreviated form large enough to accommodate one note. This is essential, for the notes on the fifth and sixth strings of the guitar are pitched below the staff and those notes on the first string, beginning with the note *G* (third fret), exceeds the upper range of the staff.

NAMES OF EXTENDED LEDGER LINES

If we begin with the top line of the staff, the first three extended ledger lines above the staff are the same name as the treble staff spaces: *F A C E*.

If we begin with the lowest line of the staff and its letter name *E*, the first three ledger lines below the staff are the treble spaces spelled backward, *E C A F*.

BAR LINES AND MEASURES

Vertical lines placed at regular intervals divide the staff into sections called a BAR, or MEASURE *(Illustration Five)*, each containing an equal number of beats. The end of a song or a section within will be marked by two adjacent vertical lines called a DOUBLE BAR line.

OCTAVE SIGN

Notes must be played an octave higher than written — on the guitar, played from a 'position' higher up the fingerboard.

STAFF: LINES and SPACES

ILLUSTRATION ONE
THE STAFF

ILLUSTRATION TWO
NOTES ON THE LINES

ILLUSTRATION THREE
NOTES ON THE SPACES

ILLUSTRATION FOUR
LEDGER LINES

ILLUSTRATION FIVE
BAR LINES AND MEASURES

OCTAVE SIGN *8va*

15

ELEMENTS OF MUSIC

OUR SYSTEM OF NOTATION

Our basic system of notation was created during the Middle Ages. This was an adaptation of the Greek system of placing "reumes", ("signs" in Greek) above the text of chants, thus indicating only the relative direction of the melody — whether a particular word or syllable should be sung higher or lower than the preceding word. This system could not incidate the actual pitch to be sung.

Before 1200, a formal system of rhythm did not exist. Later, when the need for writing definite time values became necessary, the Greek "reumes", were altered to resemble a series of straight lines and small blocks. The ▐ called "maxis" (whole tone), was the symbol for the longest note in duration. The ▐ or "longa", half as long (half note), and smaller yet, the ■ or "brevis", (quarter tone). Next the ◆ , or "semibrevis" (eighth note), and the "minima" ◆ (sixteenth note).

These forms gradually changed shape to become the symbols we now use for the whole note, half note, eighth note and sixteenth note. The thirty-second note is a modern addition.

DURATION OF NOTES (How long notes sustain)

The next thing we need to know about a note is how long it lasts, its Duration in relation to other notes. We must know the Pitch and duration before we can join notes together to create a melody.

The duration or sustain of a note is in direct relation to the beats within one Measure. Some notes sustain longer than others. The note of longest duration is the Whole Note. All other notes are exact divisions of the whole note: half note, quarter note, eighth note, sixteenth note, and the thirty-second note, Illustration One.

REST SIGNS

Music consists of silence as well as sound, and each kind of note has an equivalent Rest Sign, Illustration Five. This is the sign that is placed on the staff to indicate a note not to be played. In other words, we do not play for the amount of time that would be represented by the corresponding note.

NOTES

Symbols are written on the five line, four space staff to indicate pitch and duration of tone. These symbols are referred to as NOTES. The method of writing them is described as NOTATION. A written note provides two fundamental pieces of information: first, its placement on the staff indicates a fixed pitch; second, it provides some information, though not all, as to the length of time the note must sustain in relation to the beat.

We indicate the length of note value (how long it is to sound) by its shape; solid, hollow, with stems and/or flags *(Illustration One).* Written notes of any length can be placed high or low on the staff, written on a line, or in a space between two lines.

THE SHAPE OF NOTES

A note may be hollow or solid. It may have STEMS and FLAGS *(Illustration Two).* The color of a note, the presence of stems and flags, indicate TIME VALUE; how long the note will sustain in relation to the beat.

STEMS

You may have noticed the vertical stem placed upwards on some notes and downward on others *(Illustration Three).* The direction of the stem does not effect the pitch or length of the note value in any way. Here is the rule that governs the stem placement: Notes on the middle line of the staff, note *B*, or higher have the stems pointing DOWN. Notes below the middle line of the staff, note *B*, have the stems pointing up.

FLAGS AND BEAMS

The symbol at the end of the stem gives separate identify to each note *(Illustration Four)*, indicating NOTE VALUE, and is called a FLAG. The flag, or multiples of flags represent a further division of the quarter note. When multiples of flagged values occur together, they are commonly joined by BEAMS.

REST SIGNS

Music consists of silence as well as sound, and each kind of note has an equivalent REST SIGN *(Illustration Five).* This is the sign that is placed on the staff to indicate a note not to be played. In other words, we do not play for the amount of time that would be represented by the corresponding note.

NOTES

ILLUSTRATION ONE

DURATION OF WRITTEN NOTES (How long they sustain)

WHOLE
Four beats

HALF
Two beats

QUARTER
One beat

EIGHTH
Half a beat

SIXTEENTH
Quarter of a beat

ILLUSTRATION TWO

STEMS AND FLAGS

ILLUSTRATION THREE

BODY   **STEM**   **FLAG**   **STEP PLACED UPWARD**   **STEM PLACED DOWNWARD**

ILLUSTRATION FOUR

BEAMS

BEAM   BEAM

ILLUSTRATION FIVE

REST SIGNS

WHOLE NOTE REST   **HALF NOTE REST**   **QUARTER NOTE REST**   **EIGHTH NOTE REST**   **SIXTEENTH NOTE REST**

TABLATURE

The long process of evolution that saw the development of our "modern" musical concepts came together in the fifteenth and sixteenth centuries and still shapes our musical experience. The Italian Renaissance developed the first purely instrumental forms of music, and the six-string lute became the popular household instrumen. A special system of musical notation was developed for the instrument to aid amateur performers. Known as Tablature, this system did not directly indicate what note was to be played, but where the fingers were supposed to be placed on the frets to produce the correct notes.

Tablature is a "tool" of expediency and has many built-in shortcomings. While tablature can show where the note is on the guitar fingerboard, it does not provide for musical expression — the dynamics and duration of notes. The guitarists must know the piece being played in order to phrase it properly — how long to hold notes, how fast they should be played. Tablature is a valuable aid, but not a substitute for comprehensive music skills.

Tablature is based on a six-line staff or grid, each line representing one guitar string. The top line is the 1st (high E) string, and the bottom line represents the 6th (low E) string. The numbers that appear on the lines are fret numbers.

ACCIDENTALS (Sharps/Flats)

ACCIDENTALS *(Illustration One)* may be used to alter pitch within a measure, temporarily altering the pitch of a note. The effect of accidentals lasts only within the measure they appear.

A SHARP sign (#) before a note means to play the next fret higher in pitch. A FLAT sign (b) before a note means to play the next fret lower in pitch.

The natural sign (♮), is used to cancel a sharp or flat. Should a note which is not altered in a key signature be so designated sharp or flat in a measure, all notes written in that measure of the same alphabetical name are also altered. If it is not so marked again in the next measure, it is assumed to have returned to the normal pitch. If we want this understood, we can use the NATURAL sign which clearly indicates a return to the note's normal state at the end of the measure. To make this clearly understood, we must always use the appropriate sign.

An altered note, played sharp or flat, does not change its placement on the musical staff. The note E for example *(Illustration Two)*, remains on the bottom line of the staff regardless of whether it is written simply as E, or as E flat. The note C remains written in the third space of the staff, written as C, or as C sharp. Being aware of this will simplify your study of scales. You do not need to consider sharps and flats of the key signature when playing the appropriate fingering patterns (position, linear or zig-zag scale movements, page 54). All accidentals within the scale (key) are played, thus simplifying sight-reading.

ACCIDENTALS

ACCIDENTALS

SHARP
Raises the
pitch of any
given note by
one SEMI-TONE
(Half Step).

FLAT
Lowers the
pitch of any
given note by
one SEMI-TONE
(Half Step).

NATURAL
Restores the
note to its orig-
inal pitch, can-
celling the effect
of any previous
sharp or flat.

ILLUSTRATION TWO

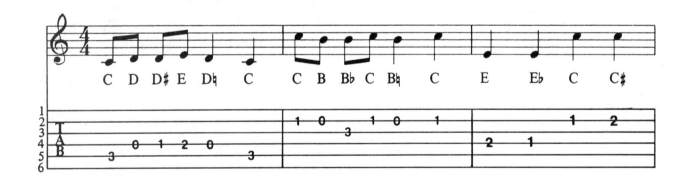

THE CONCEPT OF RHYTHM

The word RHYTHM comes from the Greek verb meaning "to flow". Rhythm is the regular beat that holds all music together, a conscious rhythm, a grouping of accents. The value of notes determine the accents, a cadence, or alternation of tension and relaxation. Rhythm must not be confused with speed. The natural rhythm of a song must remain constant. Like your heart beat, rhythm must be constant. A steady tapping of your foot is a favorite means used by musicians to express rhythmic beat.

Do you have a sense of rhythm? Do you find yourself subconsciously tapping your foot when listening to a favorite song? The ability to sense rhythm comes more naturally to some people than others. However, it can be a developed response. Practice keeping the beat to a favorite record and see if you can develop the FEEL for the rhythmic structure of the song.

DOWN BEAT — UP BEAT

The rhythmic structure of a song is expressed in BEATS. Notes are played in relation to the beat. Sound complex? It can be. However, it can also be greatly simplified. Can you tap your foot without raising it? Of course not! In order to tap your foot, you must raise your toe from the floor. This raising of the toe is called the UP BEAT *(Illustration One)*. Tap down, DOWN BEAT; raise the toe, the UP BEAT. This simple physical activity, tapping the foot, provides the structure that determines where all notes within a measure of music must be played. (The up beat is also referred to as the BACK BEAT).

The duration of all notes will be mathematically regulated to the beat, from a series of whole beats to fractions of a beat. A clock is a device used to measure regularly spaced time spans. The "second" is the basic unit which measures time. It makes possible the measurement of speed and determines the time value of any occurrence.

The BEAT in music has much the same function. It marks the regular occurrence of a pulse against which relative time value of all tones or silence is measured. The beat differs from the second in that it has no single specific duration. The beat in music can be adjusted to any speed. The speed with which the beat occurs in a musical composition is known as the TEMPO.

Any of the basic note values may be the ONE BEAT UNIT. Once the beat unit has been assigned a particular note value (quarter note, eighth note, etc.), the relationship to the other note values is measured in terms of beats. For example: If the quarter note is assigned one beat, the half note would be worth two beats; the whole note worth four beats.

TEMPO

The word TEMPO is used to express the degree of quickness or speed with which a musical composition is to be played. The tempo can be thought of as "Musical Time", a steady, even beat (tapping of the foot).

The ability to keep time, play in tempo, is a basic discipline, one that profoundly effects your playing proficiency. The tempo of a piece of music may be set fast or slow; once set, the secret is to keep it EVEN! If the tempo speeds up or slows down, it will be noticed even by the most un-musical listener. A change in tempo is more obvious than an occasional "bad" note.

Any specific tempo is measured as a number of beats per minute. Generally, the quarter note represents the beat and can be set on a metronome or electronic drum machine for a specific speed.

NOTE DIVISION

All notes are simple "multiples" of one another, or a "division" of one another. Two half notes equal the same amount of time as a whole note. Two quarter notes equal one half note. Two eighth notes equal one quarter note.

In the NOTE DIVISION CHART *(Illustration Two)*, we create one measure in 4/4 time — four beats to one measure. The whole note would be played on the first beat and sustain the full measure (one note sounded). The half note would be played on the first beat and sustain two beats. The quarter note would sustain only one beat. The eigth, sixteenth and thirty-second notes are smaller divisions of the beat.

TEMPO

During the Renaissance and Baroque periods, the human pulse was used to determine the basic measure or beat. The "metronome" was invented in 1816 by J.N. Malzel and allowed further refinement. The pendulum could be regulated to swing back and forth at a rate of 30 to 180 oscillations per minute. With the symbol ♩ M 60, for example, a composer tells the musician that the quarter note is to be played at the rate of sixty notes per minute. From this one specific time value, a musician can determine the duration of other notes (the whole note would be sounded four times as long as the quarter note). In this manner, a composer establishes the Tempo (or speed) the music is to be played.

ILLUSTRATION ONE

UP BEAT   DOWN BEAT

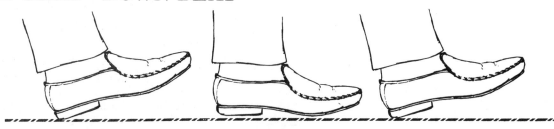

UP BEAT   **DOWN BEAT One**   **UP BEAT**

COUNT: AND . . . . . One . . . . . AND

READY   **STRUM**   **READY**

ILLUSTRATION TWO

NOTE DIVISION

	ONE		TWO		THREE		FOUR	

TIME SIGNATURES

The TIME SIGNATURE is one of the most important factors in music; it governs the rhythm to be used. In written form, the time signature is a grouping of separate numbers, one placed on top of the other in the style of a mathematical fraction without a line placed between them *(Illustration One)*.

The two numbers tell the musician how the music must be counted and how many beats there are in each measure. The TOP MEASURE represents the number of beats in each measure. The LOWER NUMBER denotes which note receives ONE COUNT (one beat).

It is important to remember that the top number refers to BEATS, not to time value. Any combination of notes or rests can be played within one measure (bar), so long as their accumulated time adds up to the total time value of the number of beats in the measure.

Time signatures are categorized in two ways: SIMPLE and COMPOUND. Simple time signatures *(Illustration Two)* give straightforward information about the type of beat and the number of beats within one measure. In simple time, the TOP NUMBER is not a multiple of three. This is the visual distinction between simple and compound time signatures.

SIMPLE TIME SIGNATURES (Common Time)

The most simple time signature (4/4) is called "four-four" time, and is often abbreviated to "C", meaning COMMON TIME. In common time, there are four beats within each measure, and each beat has the time value of one quarter note.

2/4 TIME

2/4 time has two beats within each measure with the quarter note assigned the value of one beat.

3/4 TIME

3/4 time has three beats within each measure with the quarter note assigned the value of one beat. 3/4 time is also called "Waltz Time" or "Triple Time".

COMPOUND TIME SIGNATURES

In COMPOUND time signatures *(Illustration Three)*, the top number IS a multiple of the number three. The rhythmic pulse is not felt as a SINGLE beat, but as groups of THREE beats.

Examples of Compound Time Signatures:

6/4 — Six beats per measure. Each beat is one quarter note.
6/8 — Six beats per measure. Each beat is one eighth note.
9/8 — Nine beats per measure. Each beat is one eighth note.
12/8 — Twelve beats per measure. Each beat is one eighth note.

ASYMMETRIC TIME SIGNATURES

When music has five, seven or eleven beats to each measure, it is said to be in ASYMMETRIC time, since these numbers are not divisible by two or three.

TIME SIGNATURES — METERS

Meter is the term we apply to the way in which the notes of a melody fall naturally into small groups of tones, some of which receive greater accent than others.

Accented notes may occur by making one note longer in duration than others, higher in pitch, or greater in value. Unaccented notes are often called Upbeats, *and the accented notes* Downbeats.

Common meter: 2/4, each measure containing two quarter notes; 3/4, each measure containing three quarter notes. These meters are commonly called Duple *meter and* Triple *meter.*

TIME SIGNATURES

TIME SIGNATURES

TOP NUMBER = How many beats within each measure.

BOTTOM NUMBER = The name of the note that receives one beat.

SIMPLE TIME SIGNATURES

CUT TIME

TWO BEATS PER MEASURE. EACH BEAT IS ONE QUARTER-NOTE.

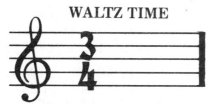

WALTZ TIME

THREE BEATS PER MEASURE. EACH BEAT IS ONE QUARTER-NOTE.

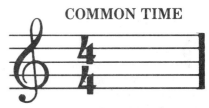

COMMON TIME

FOUR BEATS PER MEASURE. EACH BEAT IS ONE QUARTER-NOTE.

COMPOUND TIME SIGNATURES

FIVE BEATS PER MEASURE. EACH BEAT IS ONE QUARTER-NOTE.

SIX BEATS PER MEASURE. EACH BEAT IS ONE QUARTER-NOTE.

SIX BEATS PER MEASURE. EACH BEAT IS ONE EIGHTH-NOTE.

NINE BEATS PER MEASURE. EACH BEAT IS ONE EIGHTH-NOTE.

ELEVEN BEATS PER MEASURE. EACH BEAT IS ONE EIGHTH-NOTE.

TWELVE BEATS PER MEASURE. EACH BEAT IS ONE EIGHTH-NOTE.

KEY SIGNATURES

The musical scales in use at the beginning of the Renaissance (1450-1600), were based on a complicated system of church modes (scales) developed from the Greek four note Tetrachord. Since the modes during this time had been essentially intended for non-harmonic, monophonic music (single voice), they proved difficult to use in pholyony (more than one voice). A process of simplification of the whole system of toinality took place. During this time, the use of the "key signature" came into use. The key signature told the musician which note of the scale constituted the "tonal center", the basic note of the tonic chord and direction the music would have to move in order to reach a satisfying conclusion.

KEY SIGNATURES

The purpose of the key signature is to indicate the scale or key in which the music is written. It eases the eye by avoiding the placing of sharps or flats against particular notes every time they occur.

A piece of music is written in a particular KEY, which defines the PITCH or TONALITY of the scale from which the music is written. We write the key signature simply by placing the appropriate number of sharps *(Illustration One)* or flats *(Illustration Two)* at the beginning of the line. They are placed after the clef sign and before the time signature. They effect all designated notes appearing in the arrangement. You must be constantly aware of the key signature and correctly play all appropriate sharps and flats. They must not be altered in form (number or placement), unless the composer has changed keys or wishes individual notes altered. This change may be accomplished through the usage of the NATURAL sign or the placement of additional sharps or flats.

READING KEY SIGNATURES

ILLUSTRATION ONE
♯ KEYS

C

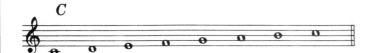

G

D

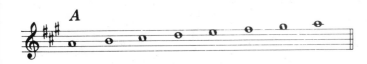

A

E

B *(sounds the same as C-flat)*

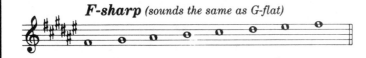

F-sharp *(sounds the same as G-flat)*

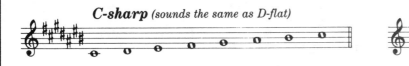

C-sharp *(sounds the same as D-flat)*

ILLUSTRATION TWO
♭ KEYS

C-flat *(sounds the same as B)*

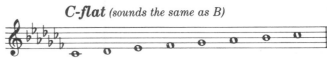

G-flat *(sounds the same as F-sharp)*

D-flat *(sounds the same as C-sharp)*

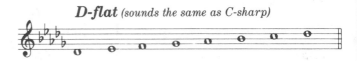

A-flat

E-flat

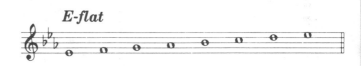

B-flat

F

C

25

ELEMENTS OF MUSIC

MELODY

Anyone can write a good MELODY. The melody of a song is what we remember; it stays in our mind, a lingering series of notes. The test of a good melody is the appeal to the listener.

In talking, our voice follows a certain CADENCE, word reflections or movements up and down in pitch, which clearly indicate whether we are merely pausing for breath, finishing a statement, asking a question or exclaiming in surprise. A melody uses similar cadences.

In its purist form, we assign a note of appropriate pitch and time value to each syllable within a word. Should a word be held in duration, rising or falling in pitch, additional notes are written to indicate the composer's intent. Syllabic division of words is made in accepted standard fashion, division or hyphenated extension of words may be shown by usage of tied notes.

Melody is a series of single tones that add up to a recognizable whole *(Illustration One)*. A melody has direction, shape and continuity. A melody has a beginning, moves up and down, conveys tension and release, expectation, arrival and has an ending. A melody may move in small intervals, or large intervals called leaps.

The melody written for instruments may have a wide range between the lowest and highest tones and often contain wide leaps and rapid notes that would be difficult to sing.

HARMONY

HARMONY occupies the main part of a study of the theory of music, a big and involved subject. In simplest terms, harmony is the sounding of two or more notes together so they blend in a pleasant or interesting way.

The history of music indicates that so long as fifteen hundred years ago, man began to write music having more than one part. We desire to hear more than one tone at a time.

The earliest form of harmony was developed by the Greeks before the Christian Era and was limited to voices singing in octaves. In the 10th Century, church musicians developed a style of music in which one voice sang a fourth or fifth note above the other. During the 11th Century, voices moved in "parallel" direction. Occasionally, they moved in opposite directions, or CONTRARY MOTION *(Illustration Two)*.

In the 12th Century, a third part was added, one voice singing the ROOT, or first note of the scale, another voice sang on the fourth and a third voice sang on the sixth note of the scale. From singing in three voices we come to the usage of the TRIAD (pronounced TRY'-AD), a three-tone chord which is the basis of music composition today.

Harmony adds support, depth and richness to the melody. A melody may be harmonized in several ways, and musicians are constantly experimenting, primarily with chords, to find supporting tones that best fit a melody's mood.

Chord progressions enrich a melody by adding emphasis and finality. The amateur musician may, incorrectly, believe that a melody is composed first and the chord structure is added later. Actually, it is most often the other way around. For example: In Jazz, repeated chord progressions are the basis of improvisation, a continually changing melody to fit the chord structure.

There are countless "rules" governing the movement of tones in relation to another. However, in simplest terms, every good melody suggests its own harmony. This ability to sense tonal movement goes beyond the scientific approach. It is the human ear that supersedes all other. If it sounds right, it *is* right.

POLYPHONY

Polyphony refers to music that has more than one melody line. These separate melodies, two or more, are called "voices", or "voice parts". Originally, polyphony music was strictly vocal. However, we now have come to think of separate melody lines, vocal or instrumental, as voices or voice parts. If we think of melody as developing a horizontal movement in time, then add another group of notes set above or below the first melody and play them simultaneously, we create a vertical or "harmonic" dimension to music. This type of music is called "counter point" (note against note). Medieval musicians called this concept "punctus contra punctum" (from Latin "ponctus") — point against point.

MELODY-HARMONY-CHORDS

ILLUSTRATION ONE

MELODY   **HARMONY**   **CHORD**

ILLUSTRATION TWO

CONTRARY MOTION

ILLUSTRATION THREE

HARMONIZED C MAJOR SCALE

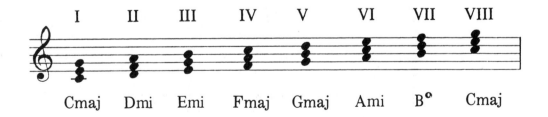

READING THE GUITAR PART
ON SHEET MUSIC

Sheet music arrangements and most song books commonly available are written for the piano. Piano arrangements are most often written on three staves. The top staff is the VOICE LINE, and will include the words. The second and third staffs are the piano arrangement. The three staves are connected with a bar line and the two piano parts are connected with an additional line called a BRACE.

Piano arrangements are often written as a solo with additional embellishments; introductions, fill-ins, breaks and harmony lines not related to the melody. Piano parts may be written with stacked notes, the lower notes harmonizing with the upper melody note.

The tonal range of the guitar encompasses the treble staff, therefore, it may be possible to play the piano treble staff part. However, this is exceedingly difficult to accomplish for it requires a great deal of skill to play double notes written for the piano. Each note written for the piano utilizes a separate key. Both notes may fall upon the same string on the guitar. An accomplished guitarist can overcome this difficulty. However, the beginner should simply play the upper note.

Most guitar song books utilize the voice line of the piano arrangement — the top staff of the standard three line piano arrangement.

NOTE: The voice line is the MELODY. It is not written as a guitar arrangement and seldom, with or without the words, is written to conform to an instrumental solo heard on records.

Popular piano arrangements most often include correct guitar chord symbols. The chords indicated may be used by the guitarist to strum the rhythm.

READING THE GUITAR PART

ILLUSTRATION ONE

VOICE LINE

PIANO RIGHT HAND

PIANO LEFT HAND

ILLUSTRATION TWO

GUITAR PART (The voice line)

TONAL RANGE OF THE GUITAR

The modern guitar has a tonal range of up to four octaves. The nylon string classic guitar (shorter neck, less frets) usually has three and a half octaves. The cutaway electric style body (24 clear frets) usually provides a two-octave range on one string.

The first obvious difference in the presentation of notes on the guitar fingerboard, as opposed to the piano keyboard, is the display (division) of the chromatic scale — the absence of the black and white keys. Both instruments are a STEPPED instrument, the key and fret dictate the pitch of the tone produced. Unlike unstepped fretless instruments such as the cello, violin and many wind instruments, the keyboard provides a visual guide. The seven white keys present the musical alphabet, *A B C D E F G*, and the five black keys, the sharps and flats. The keyboard and each string on the guitar function as a chromatic scale, however, on the guitar you cannot visually see the placement of sharps and flats.

There are both advantages and disadvantages inherent with a multi-stringed instrument. The guitar is one of the few instruments that allow you to play so many notes in so many different places.

When learning to play a piece of music on the guitar, one must first consider the position on the fingerboard that is most appropriate. It is possible to play any arrangement in several positions and you may decide to change positions while playing, since different positions produce slightly different sounds. Individual playing skill, knowledge of the fingerboard, the key in which the arrangement is written, its complexity and overall range of the tones — highest to lowest — are factors that dictate which position can be used.

The unique property of the guitar fingerboard provides the modern guitarist with ample opportunity to be self-expressive, however the creative possibilities demand that the guitarist know the instrument ... and MUSIC.

Music written expressly for the guitar is written one octave higher than it actually sounds. This may be indicated by the subscript "8", a symbol placed directly below the treble clef sign, however it is usually understood and additional symbols are not used. Writing guitar music an octave higher enables composers, with the aid of upper and lower ledger lines, to utilize one staff.

TONAL RANGE OF THE GUITAR

ILLUSTRATION ONE

PIANO

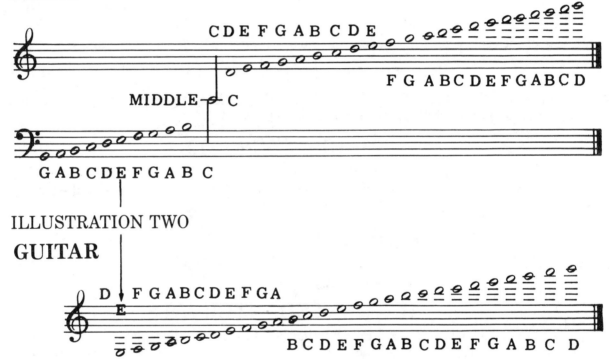

ILLUSTRATION TWO

GUITAR

ELEMENTS OF MUSIC

INTERVALS

An INTERVAL is the difference in pitch between any two notes measured in whole and half-steps. The lower tone is considered the Root or Tonic, the upper tone is the INTERVAL. When two tones of different pitch are played in succession, it is called a MELODIC INTERVAL. When two tones are played together (as in a chord), it is called an HARMONIC INTERVAL.

Intervals are identified by their position in the eight-note Diatonic Scale. They are named according to their distance from the tonic note. The first interval is called the PRIME or UNISON interval — two notes of the same letter name — two tones of the same pitch.

In the key of *C* major, the second interval is the distance between the first note and the letter *C* and the next note in the scale, the note *D*. The third interval is the distance between the first note *C*, and the third note of the scale, the note *E*. The fourth interval is the distance between the note *C* and the fourth note of the scale, the note *F*. The fifth interval is the distance between the note *C* and the fifth note of the scale, the note *G*. The sixth interval is the distance between the note *C* and the sixth note, the note *A*. The seventh interval is the distance between the letter *C* and the seventh note of the scale, the note *B*. The last interval is called the OCTAVE, the eighth note of the scale is of the same letter name as the first note, one octave apart.

PERFECT INTERVALS

When an interval is the PRIME, FOURTH, FIFTH or OCTAVE, and the upper note is of the same scale as the lower, it is called a PERFECT INTERVAL.

MINOR INTERVALS

When notes of a Major Interval are brought closer together, we have a MINOR interval. This may be accomplished by lowering the upper tone, one half-step, or raising the lower tone a half-step. The second, third, sixth and seventh intervals may be played as MINOR intervals.

DIMINISHED INTERVALS

The DIMINISHED interval is obtained by bringing a PERFECT interval or a MINOR interval one half-step closer.

AUGMENTED INTERVALS

When the interval between two tones is EXPANDED, the interval is called AUGMENTED. This applies to both the Major and Perfect intervals. Each of these become augmented by raising the upper tone one half-step, or lowering the lower tone one half-step.

TRITONE INTERVAL

The interval between the fourth and fifth is called the TRITONE. Because of the "enharmonic" spelling, the Tritone interval may be called either an "augmented" fourth, or a "diminished" fifth.

HOW TO IDENTIFY INTERVALS

When a major interval is lowered a half-step, it becomes a "minor" interval.

When a minor interval is raised by a half-step, it becomes a "major" interval.

When a major interval is raised by a half-step, it becomes an "augmented" interval.

When a minor interval is lowered by a half-step, it becomes a "diminished" interval.

When a perfect interval is raised by a half-step, it becomes an "augmented" interval.

INTERVALS

COMPOUND INTERVALS

When the second degree is an octave higher, it is called a "ninth". If it is a "major" interval naturally, it becomes a "minor", if lowered, an "augmented", if raised.

When the third degree is an octave higher, it is called a "tenth", and may be major or minor.

When the fourth degree is an octave higher, it is called an "eleventh", and can be a major, minor or augmented.

Intervals create different sound qualities. The unison, thirds, fifths, sixths and the octave create smooth, satisfying sound. These intervals are defined by the term CONSONANCE, a "soft" or "open" sound.

The second and seventh intervals create an unresolved sound, or DISSONANCE, and are called either "sharp" or "mild".

The tritone (fourth) has an ambiguous quality and may be either consonant or dissonant.

INTERVAL INVERSIONS

When intervals are INVERTED, the tonal quality of either consonance or dissonance may change. This is because the register (tonal range) of the two notes, and the spacing between them, has been altered.

An interval is said to be "inverted" when the lower note becomes the higher, or the higher note becomes the lower. This may be accomplished by raising the lower note an octave, or by lowering the higher note one octave.

INTERVALS AND CHORDS (TRIADS)

Intervals are the building blocks of chords. Intervals, when combined in a specific, vertical relationship produce a TRIAD (the simultaneous sounding of three notes). Example: C Major Chord; Root, C; plus the "third" and "fifth" above the Root. This combination forms a triad of TWO intervals, each a third.

There are four kinds of triads: Major, Minor, Augmented and Diminished. Although the intervals that make up the triad are always thirds, they may be either Major or Minor thirds, and may appear in different vertical order.

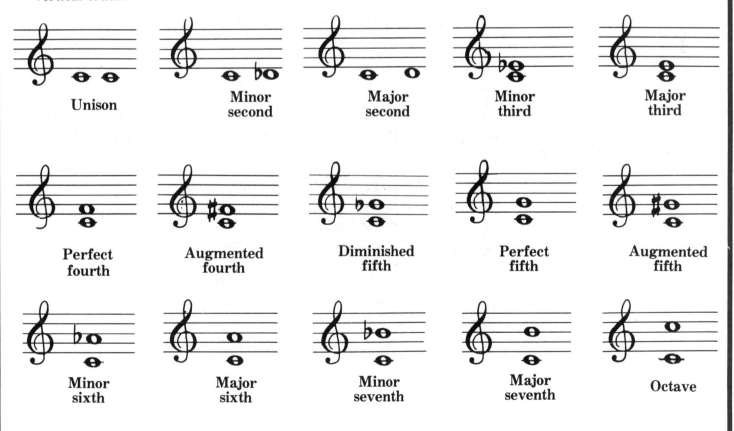

Unison   Minor second   Major second   Minor third   Major third

Perfect fourth   Augmented fourth   Diminished fifth   Perfect fifth   Augmented fifth

Minor sixth   Major sixth   Minor seventh   Major seventh   Octave

CADENCE — CHORD HARMONY

Renaissance composers learned to organize their music in terms of Cadences or Cadential Formulas, a short group of chords used as an end or point of arrival from the melody.

In the late Renaissance and the late Baroque period, which lasted from about 1600 to 1750, the polyphony style of music changed. The use of the "middle-range" voices was discarded. One voice, in the "treble register", was to become responsible for carrying the melody. Composers of this period discovered that certain combinations of three notes produced the most sonorous types of support for the high range, single voice melody, and gave the whole piece of music a firm sense of movement. These three tones with the interval of third between the two and the tonal interval from the top note to the fifth, was called a "chord triad".

CADENCE

During the development of diatonic harmony in the eighteenth and nineteenth centuries, rules were established to govern the movement of one chord to another. The foremost function was to organize chord changes within a key, so that the tonic chord emerged clearly as the ROOT, or "home chord".

While a chord can be built on each note of a scale, chords built upon the Tonic I, Sub-Dominant IV and Dominant V, came to be called the PRIMARY CHORDS. Their importance was determined by what is called CADENCE (from the Latin word meaning "to fall"). The cadence is a concluding phrase, or a phrase suggesting finality or conclusion. A cadence normally occurs at or near the end of a melody or section of music.

Our ear is trained to hear natural cadences in music and language. "I would continue, however …". "Why don't you …". These are examples of language cadence. They clearly let us know these sentences are incomplete. The sentence: "Well … maybe", has a partial finality. "I said to stop!", is an example of complete resolution, a solid statement upon which to end.

Chord movement reflects a definite sense of either motion, tension or resolution. There are four different cadences in primary chord progressions: PERFECT CADENCE, IMPERFECT CADENCE, PLAGAL CADENCE and INTERRUPTED CADENCE.

PERFECT CADENCE is the resolution from the Dominant (V) to the Tonic (I) chord. When we hear this cadence, for example in the key of C Major, the Dominant Seventh (G7) demands resolution. Our ear tells us we must move to a point of rest, and the movement to the Tonic chord C Major, brings the resolution to a stopping point. The I chord is the "home tone", the most common chord used; it denotes complete resolution, a point of rest. The Dominant (V) chord is the next most frequently used and influential chord in music. The construction of the Dominant Seventh chord, a major third plus a minor seventh creates a unique tonality which to our ear cannot stand alone, but demands resolution. The Dominant Seventh is a four-tone chord and blends perfectly in any key major or minor.

IMPERFECT CADENCE is the progression from the Tonic (I) chord to the Dominant (V) chord. It normally occurs in the middle of a chord sequence, not at the end. The movement of the II, IV or VI to the Dominant is also considered an IMPERFECT CADENCE.

PLAGAL CADENCE is the resolution from the Sub-Dominant (IV) to the Tonic (I).

INTERRUPTED CADENCE is the resolution from the Dominant (V) chord to any chord other than the Tonic (I), usually to the III, IV or VI chord.

BASIC RULES OF CHORD HARMONY

The basic rules of traditional harmony create a system of how chords built upon notes of the diatonic scale should be used in establishing a chord progression.

● The TONIC (I) chord can resolve to any chord.

● The SUPER TONIC (II) chord can resolve to any chord except the Tonic (I).

● The MEDIANT (III) chord can resolve to any chord except the Tonic or Leading Tone (VII) chord.

● The SUB-DOMINANT (IV) chord can resolve to any chord.

● The DOMINANT (V) chord can resolve to any chord except the II or VII.

● The SUB-MEDIANT (VI) chord can resolve to any chord except the I or VII.

● The LEADING TONE (VII) chord can resolve to any chord except the II or IV.

● The fundamental rules of chord progression revolve around the two strongest chords: the Tonic (I), and the Dominant (V).

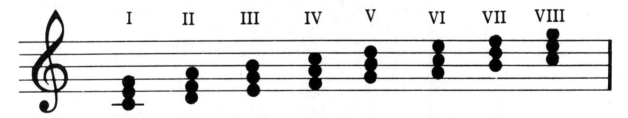

	I	II	III	IV	V	VI	VII	VIII
CHORDS	C MAJ	D MI	E MI	F MAJ	G MAJ	A MI	B°	C MAJ

CADENCE —
CHORD HARMONY
Renaissance composers learned to
organize their music in terms of
CADENCE or CADENTIAL
FORMULAS; a short group of
chords used as an end or point of
arrival from the melody.

THE THREE-CHORD PROGRESSION THEORY

A chord may be built upon each note of the diatonic scale. A chord is the simultaneous sounding of three or more tones, a TRIAD. From the many chords available in a given key, three have come to represent the basic rhythm movement around which much of our modern "commercial" music has evolved. These three chords are called the PRIMARY CHORDS. They always sound good together and define the tonal movement of the arrangement.

In usage, the TONIC (I) chord, built on the first note of the scale, sets the pitch, or the key in which the song is played. The SUBDOMINANT (IV) chord, built on the fourth note of the scale, sounds higher than the tonic chord. The DOMINANT (V) chord, built on the fifth note of the scale and placed higher in the scale, should sound higher, but is often inverted or played from a position so as to sound lower than the tonic chord.

To improve resolution back to the tonic chord (the natural movement within a chord progression), the dominant chord is usually played as a DOMINANT SEVENTH chord. Example: Key of *C*; (I) *C*, (IV) *F*, (V) *G7*.

THREE-CHORD PROGRESSION

THE THREE-CHORD PROGRESSION
(The More Common Keys)

	PRIMARY CHORDS			RELATIVE MINOR CHORDS		
Key	I Tonic	IV Sub-Dom	V Dominant	II	III	VI
C	C	F	G₇	Dm	Em	Am
D	D	G	A₇	Em	F#m	B
E	E	A	B₇	F#	G#	C#
F	F	Bb	C₇	Gm	Am	Dm
G	G	C	D₇	Am	Bm	Em
A	A	D	E₇	Bm	C#m	F#m
B	B	E	F#	C#m	D#m	G#m

THE STRUCTURE OF SCALES

By the early sixteenth century, music began moving away from the earlier Greek Modes — scale played only on the pure alphabet: A B C D E F G. These older forms of scales, each with it's own step, half-step pattern, in their simplicity, were too confining for the emergence of "polyphone" music. By the seventeenth century, the new concept of "tonality" was perfected and the Key System as we now know it became the modern musical form.

The scale is a predetermined, logical series of notes combined within a specific pattern suitable for harmony. The scale structure is based on the placement of tones and semi-tones (English terminology), or whole-steps and half-steps (American terminology).

The characteristic sound of any scale is determined by its number of tones, the order in which they occur, and by their size — if the sistance is a step or a half-step.

The distance between notes remains constant, the Interval between notes is fixed and will not change, even if the music is played in another key. In this manner, we recognize a song and can hum the melody regardless of the key (pitch) in which it is performed, making it possible to transpose a piece of music to different keys.

The sound of the Major Diatonic Scale is due to the placement of the half-steps between the 3rd and 4th notes and between the 7th and 8th notes. The resulting two-tone (step, step), interval between the 1st and 3rd notes create the scales Major *characteristic.*

WHAT IS A MAJOR DIATONIC SCALE?

A chromatic scale is the progression, in half-steps, of all twelve musical notes with the thirteenth note repeating the first note an octave higher. Most modern music is not written with the chromatic scale, but reduced to the more pleasant-sounding eight note DIATONIC SCALE.

The Major Diatonic Scale is a predetermined pattern of eight notes arranged in five whole steps (whole tones) and two half-steps (semi-tones). A whole step is equal to TWO frets on the guitar and a half-step is the distance of ONE fret. In other words, a Major Diatonic Scale is a succession of tones arranged in a fixed step, step, half-step pattern. We hear this as a natural progression of tones when played on any musical instrument.

A diatonic scale may be built commencing on any of the twelve notes of the chromatic scale. Thus, we have twelve major scales called KEYS, each a different pitch. The diatonic scale covers the same tonal range as the chromatic scale of the same name. However, it is made up of only eight of the chromatic scale's thirteen notes. In order to eliminate the unwanted notes from the chromatic scale, we use the STEP, STEP, HALF-STEP, principal *(Illustration One)*. Again, a step is the distance of TWO frets on the guitar.

THE *C* DIATONIC MAJOR SCALE IN WRITTEN FORM

Illustration Two represents the *C* Major Diatonic Scale as it appears in written notation.

NOTES ON THE FINGERBOARD THE *C* MAJOR SCALE

Experiment with the step, step, half-step, step, step, step, half-step principle on the guitar. Start at any fret and walk up the fingerboard using the correct step, half-step pattern *(Illustration Three)*. Your ending note should always be the same letter name as your starting note. In playing this scale pattern, use all four fingers — starting with the first finger on the first note.

THE DIATONIC SCALE

ILLUSTRATION ONE

THE MAJOR DIATONIC SCALE: Seven notes

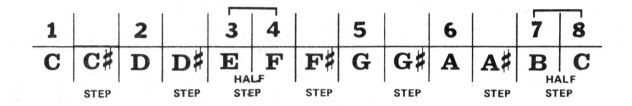

ILLUSTRATION TWO

C MAJOR DIATONIC SCALE-WRITTEN FORM

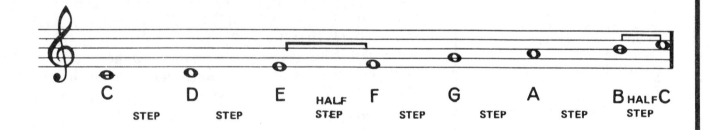

ILLUSTRATION THREE

C SCALE NOTES ON THE GUITAR FINGERBOARD

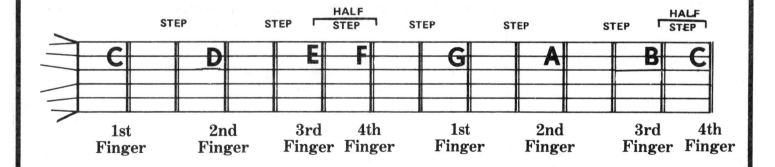

Definition of the scale degree names:

(I) Tonic. *The sound from which the scale takes its tonality and name.*
(II) Supertonic. *Superior above; the degree above the tonic.*
(III) Mediant. *The mediant lies midway between the two most important sounds of the scale — the first (tonic) and the fifth (dominant).*
(IV) Sub-Dominant. *The Sub-Dominant (fourth degree) is under the dominant, the fifth degree.*
(V) Dominant. *The fifth degree generates a dominating character. After the tonic, it is the strongest note in the key.*
(VI) Sub-Mediant. *It occupies the same position below the upper tonic (8th note of the scale — the octave note), as the mediant does above the tonic.*
(VII) Leading Tone. *It leads the ear to expect and anticipate the sounds of the key (tonic) note.*

THE SCALE IN THEORETICAL FORM
(ILLUSTRATION ONE)

Each note of the Diatonic Scale is commonly called DEGREE, however, there are other terms that may be applied to each note of the scale.

ARABIC NUMERALS: Each degree may be shown as an Arabic numeral: 1 2 3 4 5 6 7 8.

ROMAN NUMERALS: Each degree may be shown as a Roman numeral: I II III IV V VI VII VIII.

THE DO RE MI SYSTEM: In 1812, Sara Ann Glover developed the SO-FA system to enable vocalists to sing the notes of the Diatonic Scale (DO being the first or TONIC note of the scale).

THEORETICAL FORM: The correct theoretical name for each degree of the scale (TONIC, SUPER TONIC, MEDIANT, DOMINANT, SUB-DOMINANT, SUB-MEDIANT, LEADING TONE, TONIC) is commonly used in chord theory studies and is often used on rhythm charts to indicate chord names in given keys.

THE DIATONIC SCALE EXTENDED TWO OCTAVES
(ILLUSTRATION TWO)

The Major Diatonic Scale (eight notes) may be continued on in higher or lower sequences called OCTAVES. It is permissible to continue counting numerically (9 10 11 12 13 14 15) to determine the next octave. The first and eighth are the same alphabetically, as are the second and ninth, third and tenth.

When building EXTENDED chords (9th, 11th, 13th) this continuation of the scale is utilized to determine these additional notes *(Illustration Three)*.

THE DIATONIC SCALE

ILLUSTRATION ONE

C MAJOR SCALE: Theoretical form

ALPHABETICAL	C	D	E	F	G	A	B	C
ARABIC	**1**	**2**	**3**	**4**	**5**	**6**	**7**	**8**
ROMAN	I	II	III	IV	V	VI	VII	VIII
SOL-FA	**DO**	**RE**	**MI**	**FA**	**SOL**	**LA**	**TI**	**DO**
THEORETICAL	TONIC	SUPER TONIC	MEDIANT	SUB DOM	DOMINANT	SUB MEDIANT	LEADING TONE	TONIC
INTERVALS	PERFECT PRIME	MAJOR SECOND	MAJOR THIRD	PERFECT FOURTH	PERFECT FIFTH	MAJOR SIXTH	MAJOR SEVENTH	PERFECT OCTAVE
ABBREVIATIONS	(P.P.)	(Ma 2)	(Ma 3)	(P. 4)	(P. 5)	(Ma 6)	(Ma 7)	(P. 8)

ILLUSTRATION TWO

THE DIATONIC SCALE EXTENDED TWO OCTAVES

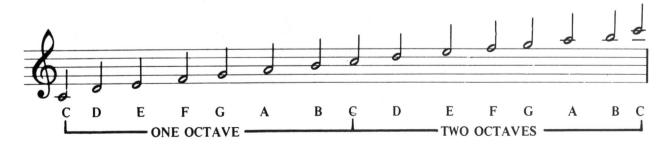

ILLUSTRATION THREE

C MAJOR SCALE EXTENDED TWO OCTAVES

STANDARD TUNING
AND THE CHROMATIC SCALE

INTERVALS OF TUNING. There are many ways the guitar may be tuned, and each tuning changes the placement and pitch of the notes at each fret. Over the years, the *E A D G B E* (6th through 1st string) has become STANDARD TUNING *(Illustration One)*. Tuning establishes the difference or INTERVAL between each string. Five strings are tuned a fourth interval apart (*E* to *A*, *A* to *D*, *E* to *G*, *B* to *E*, respectively). The third to second string is tuned a 3rd interval (*G* to *B*).

Once the individual string has been accurately tuned to proper pitch, the establishment of the chromatic scale of that string has been set in place. Fretting a string will produce a tone predictable in pitch and alphabetical name. Simply knowing the note produced by plucking the "open string", provides the knowledge to quickly determine the note produced at each fret. Start with the open string note and run through the chromatic scale! The notes on the twelfth fret have the same names as the notes of the open string, one octave higher.

PLAYING THE *A* CHROMATIC SCALE. How difficult is it to play the chromatic scale? How quickly may it be played? Pluck the open 6th string (note *E*). Press the string down on the first fret and slide your finger along the fingerboard, stopping on the twelfth fret (the note *E* one octave higher). You will have played the *E* Chromatic Scale *(Illustration Two)*.

Let us examine another way the chromatic scale may be played. Obviously, we can play all notes on one string *(Illustration Two, a LINEAR movement)*. We may also play across the strings: Start with the open 6th string, note *E*, and play *E F F*# *G G*#; then play the next note, note *A*, on the open 5th string and continue — *A A*# *B C C*#, fourth fret, then play the next note, open string *D; D D*# *E*, completing the *E* chromatic scale — one octave *(Illustration Three)*.

There are many variations possible and a thorough study should be made for it provides an excellent way to better understand the complexities of the fingerboard. All scales (chromatic, diatonic, diminished, augmented and whole-tone, for example) are essentially just different ways of dividing the octave into whole and half-step patterns.

The tuning fork, a two-pronged steel rod tuned to a fixed rate of vibration is a device that unlike electronic instruments, will last a lifetime. When struck, it vibrates and produces a precise frequency. It is possible to purchase a tuning fork that produces the exact pitch of each string of the guitar.

The British Standards Institution, in 1939, adopted the frequency of 440 cycles per second as standard pitch for the tone A *above middle C. This became known as standard pitch. The A 440 tuning fork is most commonly used to tune the guitar.*

The A 440 pitch of the tuning fork is produced on the guitar at the fifth fret-first string. This tone is two octaves above the tone of the open fifth string (the A *string). However, it is easy to match the open* A *string to the tone of the tuning fork. With this one string tuned to pitch, the other strings may be tuned by matching tones across the strings.*

TUNING AND THE CHROMATIC SCALE

ILLUSTRATION ONE

INTERVAL OF TUNING

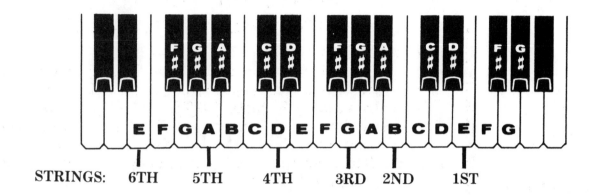

ILLUSTRATION TWO

PLAYING THE E CHROMATIC SCALE (6th strings)

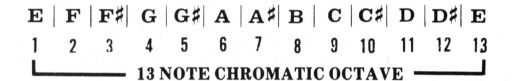

ILLUSTRATION THREE

LINEAR MOVEMENT — CHROMATIC SCALE

OPEN POSITION — ACROSS THE FINGERBOARD

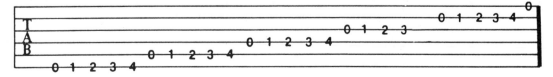

ELEMENTS OF MUSIC

Western Music is "polyphonetic music", more than one melody, and we have been conditioned to expect melody and harmony — a beginning, middle and an end — to our modern music. As a general rule, the chromatic scale, based on the division of the octave into twelve intervals — twelve half-steps, dominates our music. In other cultures, the octave has been divided into smaller intervals. Example: The Arabic octave is divided into seventeen parts. The Greeks developed the four-tone Tetrachord; the pentatonic, five-tone scale is of ancient Chinese, Scottish and African origin. Musicians of the Medieval Europe used a six-tone hexachord scale.

TETRACHORDS

The Diatonic Major Scale can be best described by using the word TETRACHORD (from the Greek "Tetra", meaning four; and the Latin "Corda", meaning notes). A tetrachord consists of a series of four successive notes written in a given pattern which is fixed in position and will not alter in form. It is comprised of two whole steps and one half-step (step, step, half-step, *Illustration One*).

TETRACHORD FORMULATION OF SHARPS. The Major Diatonic Scale is constructed with two overlapping tetrachords separated by a whole step *(Illustration Two)*. The first or TONIC note of the first tetrachord establishes the key, the second tetrachord is built upon the 5th (dominant) note. In building scales, the second tetrachord adds an additional accidental to each new key. Each key progresses from the 5th tone of the previous scale (a device called the "circle of dominants, or the CIRCLE OF FIFTHS). If we would continue writing tetrachords in this manor, we would progress naturally through what is also called the CYCLE OF KEYS, returning to the key of *C* Major *(Illustration Three)*. Ascending tetrachords, starting with *C* Major, create the SHARP keys.

TETRACHORD FORMULATION OF FLAT KEYS. When writing scales in descending motion, the tetrachord movement is reversed (half-step, step, step). Each additional tetrachord, in descending order commences on the fourth degree (sub-dominant) of the scale, moving in descending CYCLE OF FOURTHS. Descending tetrachords starting with *C* Major create the FLAT keys.

TETRACHORDS

ILLUSTRATION ONE

THE TETRACHORD

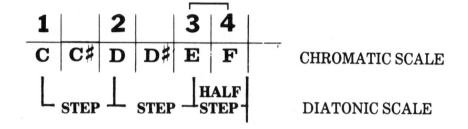

ILLUSTRATION TWO

C MAJOR DIATONIC SCALE-TWO TETRACHORDS

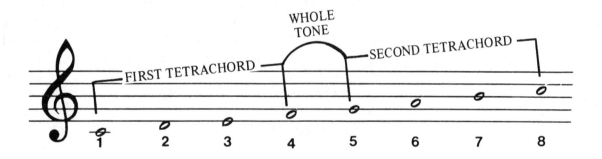

ILLUSTRATION THREE

OVERLAPPING TETRACHORDS

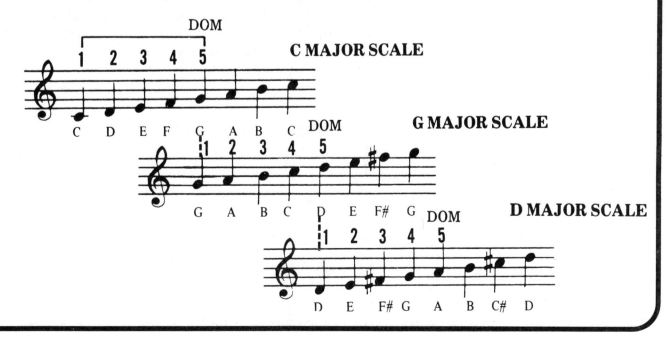

ELEMENTS OF MUSIC

PRIMARY CHORDS TO EACH KEY

If we choose any chord around the circle and make it our key (tonic) chord, and then use the chord on either side of it, we would have the three primary chords of the key of the first chord chosen — the TONIC (I), the SUB-DOMINANT (IV) and the DOMINANT (V).

In *Illustration One*, we have chosen the key of *C* Major, and the *C* tonic chord. The Dominant Chord in the key of *C* Major is the chord *G*, shown to the right of *C* and the Sub-Dominant chord is the chord on the left of *C*, the *F* chord.

CIRCLE OF 5ths-CIRCLE OF 4ths

Counting clockwise, the keys move in 5ths (count up five letters in the musical alphabet). This movement is known as the circle of 5ths, a movement from the One chord, the Tonic, to the Five chord, the Dominant.

RELATED MINOR CHORDS

Illustration Three shows the Related Minor chords to each major chord. By utilizing the Circle of Fifths, you can easily find the six basic chords to any key — the Tonic, Sub-Dominant, Dominant, and the three related minor chords.

FORMULA FOR FINDING 3 PRIMARY CHORDS
FORMULA 1 4 5

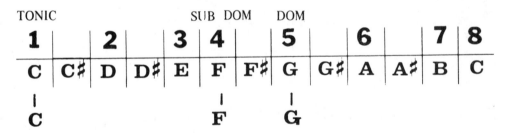

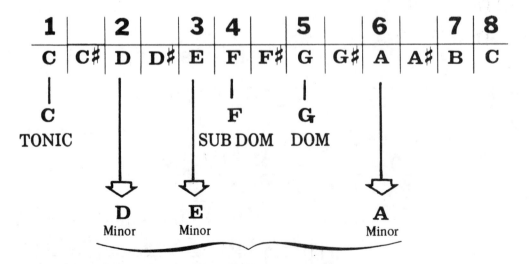

RELATIVE MINOR CHORDS TO THE KEY OF C

CIRCLE OF KEYS-MODULATION

ILLUSTRATION ONE

CIRCLE OF KEYS

4ths flat)   5ths sharp

MODULATION IN 5ths

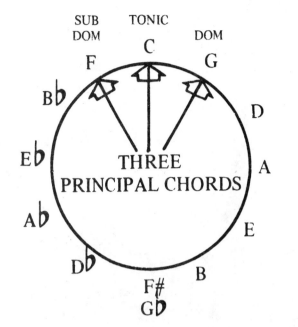

ILLUSTRATION TWO

CIRCLE OF 5ths-CIRCLE OF 4ths

4ths (Flat)   5ths (Sharp)

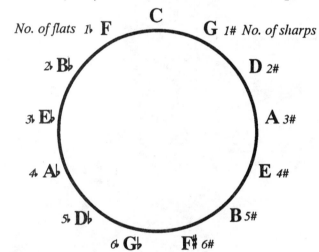

ILLUSTRATION THREE

RELATED MINOR CHORDS

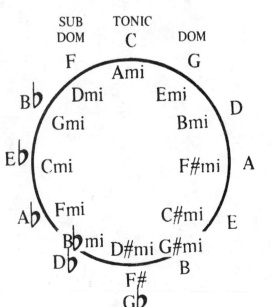

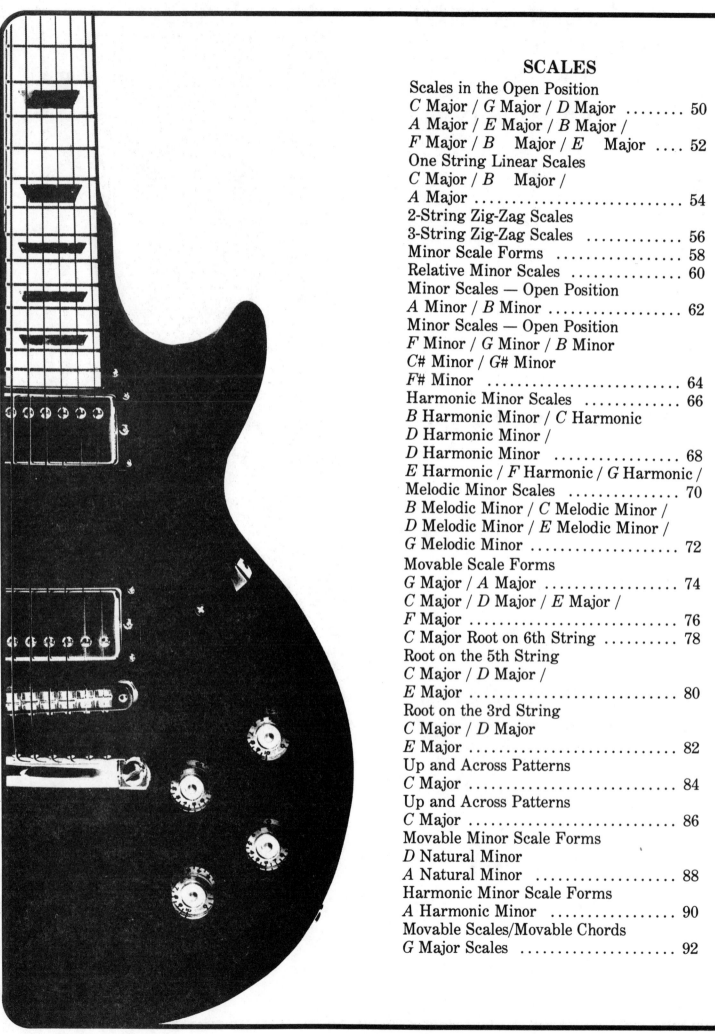

SCALES

SCALES
SCALES
SCALES
SCALES
SCALES
SCALES
SCALES
SCALES
SCALES
SCALES
SCALES
SCALES
SCALES
SCALES
SCALES
SCALES
SCALES
SCALES
SCALES
SCALES

SCALE POSITIONS

The interpretation of written music and its performance on the guitar requires THREE skills: First, you must be able to read music (identify notes by name); second, you must be familiar with the guitar fingerboard and know instinctively where each note should be played; third, you must have developed the physical skills (hand dexterity), to promptly fret the correct note.

It is possible to play scales (melodies) on one string, a "linear" movement, ascending and descending in pitch. However, this requires extensive hand movement and increases the chance of playing errors. To play a diatonic scale would encompass thirteen frets. We may also play a "zig-zag" movement, playing up and down the fingerboard and across strings. And, we have the position. A POSITION is generally considered to be a portion of the fingerboard that encompasses six frets, allowing you to play scales across the fingerboard, moving across the strings. Playing a fixed position reduces hand movement and helps eliminate playing errors.

There are two types of positions possible on the guitar fingerboard: the OPEN position and the CLOSED position. The open position is considered to be the notes of the open strings and all notes within the first four frets. A closed position (no open string notes) implies a specified fixed position on the fingerboard covering a range of six frets, across all six strings and utilizes a four finger movement.

THE OPEN POSITION. The usual starting place, as taught in most guitar method books, is the open string position. In the open position, the notes produced by the un-fretted strings function for notes that, in a closed position, would require first and fourth finger stretches to fret.

The open position offers many possibilities to add hammer-ons and pull-offs, especially in the keys of *E A D* and *G* major. Bluegrass and finger style guitarists make extensive usage of the open position scales, utilizing the open string's tendency to ring after it has been played.

The open string position produces every note of the chromatic scale and, in the key of *E* Major, covers two octaves. In the open position, each note of the chromatic scale has only one fingering/one location, except the note *B*, open second string, which may also be played on the 3rd string 4th fret.

PLAYING THE OPEN STRING POSITION. Each "open string" diagram places all playable notes of each individual scale within the open position. The complete octave (or in some instances, two octaves) is shown. A black check-mark underlines the ROOT or tonic note. Practice playing the entire scale from the lowest note possible through the highest, not just from the root note.

The open position lends itself to the keys of *C* Major, its related minor scales, and the sharp keys: *G D A* and *E* Major, and their related minor scales. The key of *F* Major — one flat, plays easily in the open position. However, most "flat" keys do not finger easily and for the most part are seldom played from the open position.

TABLATURE is a number system of writing music for the guitar and other stringed instruments. Guitar tablature utilizes a six-line grid — each line representing a guitar string. The top line represents the first string, the bottom line the sixth string. The numbers placed on the lines represent the correct fret to be played. The O represents the "open strings".

SCALES IN THE OPEN POSITION

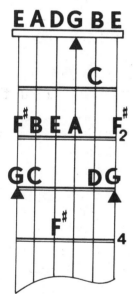

E A D G B E

F   C F

B   E A   2

G C F   D G

B   4

* *Optional Fingering*

C MAJOR SCALE Open position

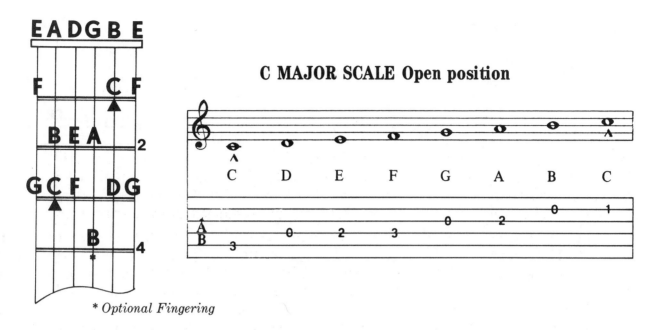

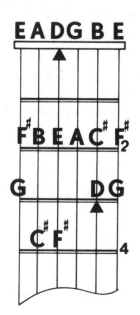

E A D G B E

C

F#   B E A   F#2

G C   D G

F#   4

G MAJOR SCALE Open position (Two Octaves)

E A D G B E

F# B E A C# F#2

G   D G

C# F#   4

D MAJOR SCALE Open position

SCALES

A MAJOR SCALE Open position

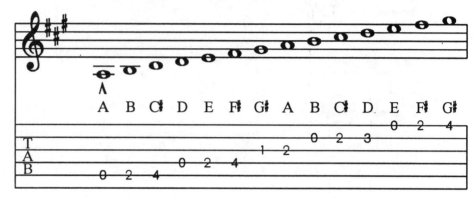

E MAJOR SCALE Open position (Two Octaves)

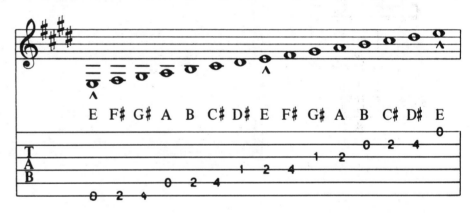

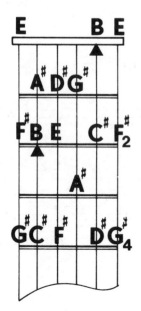

B MAJOR SCALE Open position

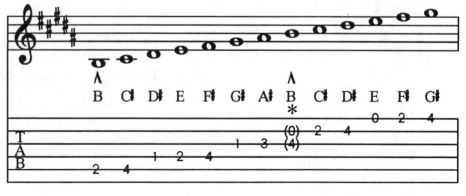

*Optional Fingering

SCALES IN THE OPEN POSITION

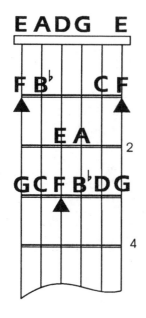

F MAJOR SCALE Open position (Two Octaves)

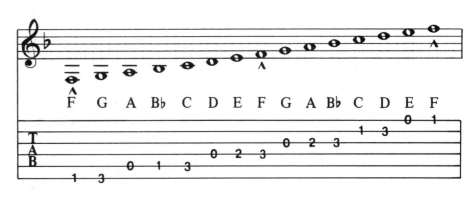

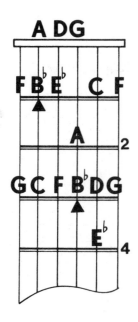

B♭ MAJOR SCALE Open position (Bb)

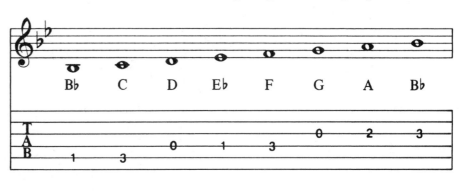

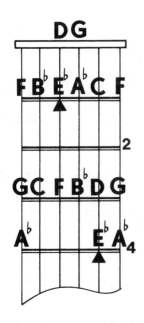

E♭ MAJOR SCALE Open position (Eb)

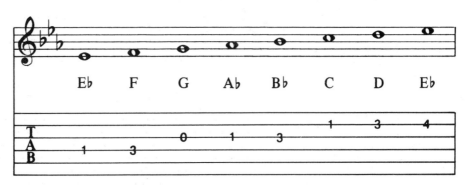

MAJOR SCALE FINGERING PATTERNS

ONE STRING LINEAR MOVEMENT. Playing a major scale on one string clearly transposes the step, step, half-step movement of the Tetrachord to the guitar fingerboard in a visual pattern not so easily recognizable when the scale is played from a position. Playing a linear movement provides an opportunity to not only practice left-hand fingering movements, but we can also clearly hear the intervals of the major scale.

Practice playing the linear movement, commencing on any fret and string you desire. The placement of the first finger — the first note played — will be the TONIC or KEY note. Example: If you begin on the note *C (Illustration One)*, you will play the *C* Major Scale. Use all four fingers, walk up the fingerboard ascending, down the fingerboard descending. Learn to quickly and accurately shift the hand, enabling the first finger to play the 5th note ascending, and the 4th finger descending. This left-hand fingering with a one-fret shift illustrates the Major Scale Tetrachord formation; two tetrachords, separated by a whole step, one fret — the "shift".

ILLUSTRATION ONE

C MAJOR Linear scale

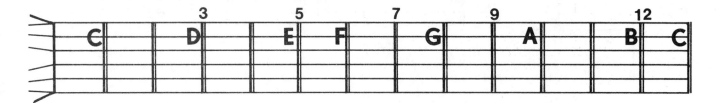

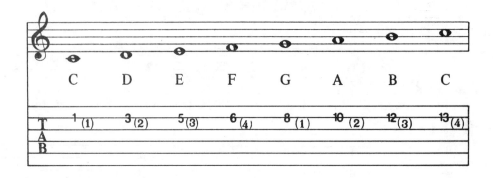

ONE STRING LINEAR SCALE

B♭ MAJOR Linear scale (Bb)

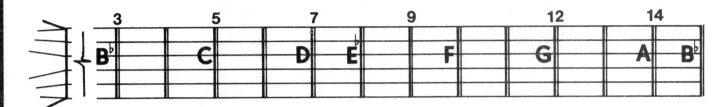

A MAJOR Linear scale

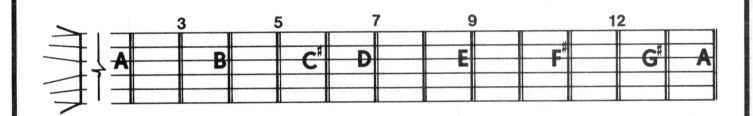

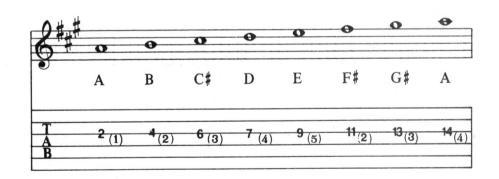

SCALES

TWO-STRING ZIG-ZAG MOVEMENT

When practicing the one-string linear scale movement, you realize the limitation of playing melodies on only one string — too much hand movement. It requires infinite practice to acquire the ability to shift smoothly and play each note evenly — almost impossible at fast tempo. Occasionally, the one-string scale movement can be used effectively, and should be practiced. However, the same results can be achieved without the bothersome "shift".

In *Illustration One*, we again have the *C* major scale, starting on the fifth string, third fret, and following through with the first Tetrachord finger movement, ending with the fourth finger playing the note *F*, eighth fret. Now, we move over to the fourth string, fifth fret — first finger, to play the next note in the scale, note *G*, the first finger of the second Tetrachord movement; finishing with the fourth finger playing the note *C*, fourth string, tenth fret.

In *Illustration Two*, we play the *C* scale starting the first Tetrachord on the note *C*, 3rd string. Practice this scale using the proper fingering — stepping through the first four-note Tetrachord, shift over to the next string and play the second Tetrachord.

Want to learn dozens of scales? Each finger movement shown in these two illustrations are "closed" positions — they incorporate no open strings, therefore each position (scale) is movable. Start the same finger pattern one fret higher and you will correctly play a C# scale. One fret higher and the first note becomes *D*, and you will be playing a *D* Major Scale.

This finger pattern will correctly produce the major scale anywhere on the fingerboard beginning with any fret on any string with one important exception: The 3rd interval tuning between the third and second string (all other strings are a 4th interval apart) requires a two-fret adjustment when moving across the third and second string *(Illustration Two)*.

Any scale pattern (fingering) chosen should allow for tone clarity, fingering accuracy, and playing proficiency. Linear movement can often be beneficial and should be practiced. It is important to strive for THE LEAST AMOUNT of hand movement.

ZIG ZAG SCALES

ILLUSTRATION ONE

C MAJOR 2 string zig zag

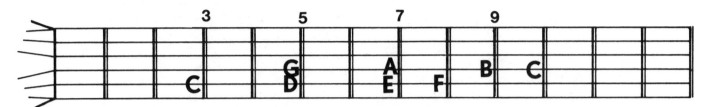

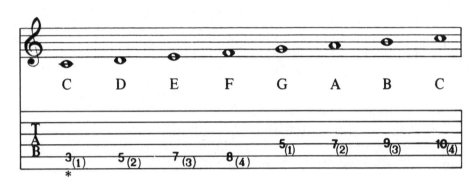

*
*(1) numbers placed within parenthese indicates correct fingering.

ILLUSTRATION TWO

C MAJOR SCALE 2 string zig zag

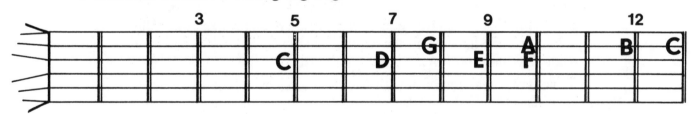

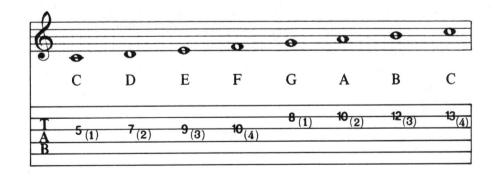

SCALES

MINOR SCALE FORMS

MINOR (meaning "lesser" or "smaller"). The minor scale, formerly "the scale with the lesser third", was developed in the seventeenth century from the Greek Aeolian and Dorian modes. While the major scale is said to have a "bright-lively" character, the minor has a "sad" connotation, often thought of as the "Russian" sound.

There are three forms of the diatonic minor scale: NATURAL minor, HARMONIC minor and MELODIC minor. Each has its own individual step, half-step pattern, and each has a different sound and musical application. They all share one common feature that differentiates them from the Diatonic Major Scale: Minor scales have a "flat" third. The interval between the first and third notes in the scale is a step and half, this is called a MINOR THIRD. The three minor scales (with a flat 3rd) differ from each other only in the placement of their sixth and seventh tones. The Harmonic and Melodic are altered Natural minor scales.

The natural minor scale shares the same key signature as a major scale and utilizes the same notes indicated by the Key Signature, those notes determined by that key signature's Diatonic Major Scale.

The natural minor scale has one flaw or deviation from the accepted rules of modern harmony. The whole tone (one step) between the 6th and 7th notes will not permit the building of a Dominant 7th chord, the pivotal chord in modern chord harmony, the chord necessary to achieve a PERFECT CADENCE. In order to overcome this problem when formulating chord progressions, the 7th note of the natural minor scale is raised by a half-step. The new scale is called the HARMONIC MINOR.

This new placement of the 7th and 8th note, now a half-step apart, increases the distance between the 6th and 7th note to three half-steps (a minor third). When writing melody lines, this is an unacceptably large interval. The solution to this problem is to raise the 6th note of the scale by a half-step. The result is a smoother melody flow. This procedure, used when ascending in pitch, is called the MELODIC MINOR. When playing a descending melody, the interval between the melodic minor 6th and 7th notes is reduced to a half-step, providing a smoother melodic flow. This creates the NATURAL MINOR scale.

58

MINOR SCALE FORMS

ILLUSTRATION ONE

MAJOR THIRD INTERVAL

MINOR THIRD INTERVAL

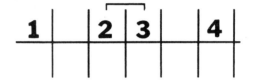

ILLUSTRATION TWO

THE NATURAL MINOR SCALE

THE HARMONIC MINOR SCALE

THE MELODIC MINOR SCALE Ascending

THE MELODIC MINOR SCALE Descending

RELATIVE MINOR SCALE *C* MAJOR

The Greek IONIAN MODE was the predecessor of the Major Diatonic Scale. The natural minor is derived from the Greek AEOLIAN MODE. In the key of *C* Major, the Ionian scale begins on the letter *C* and the Aeolian minor scale commences on the letter *A*, the sixth note of the scale.

The Diatonic Major Scale and its Relative Minor Scale share the same key signature and share the same notes. Because each scale starts at a different place within the scale, the step, step-half placement is dissimilar and each scale produces a contrasting sound. In *Illustration One*, we show how the *A* Minor scale is derived from the *C* Major scale.

RELATIVE MINOR SCALE

ILLUSTRATION ONE

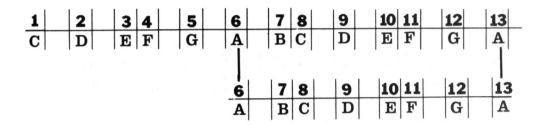

C MAJOR

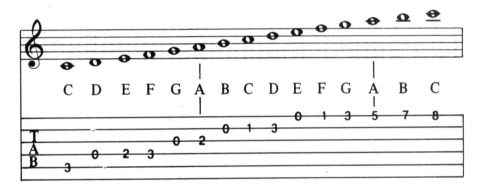

A NATURAL MINOR

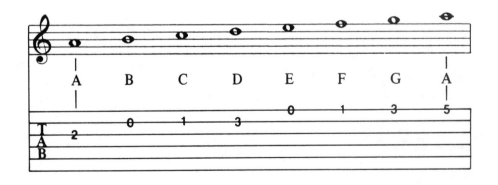

PLAYING MINOR SCALES
IN THE OPEN POSITION

Each "open string" diagram places all playable notes of each individual minor scale within the open position. The complete octave (or in some instances, two octaves) is shown and indicated by the black check-mark marking the ROOT (tonic) note.

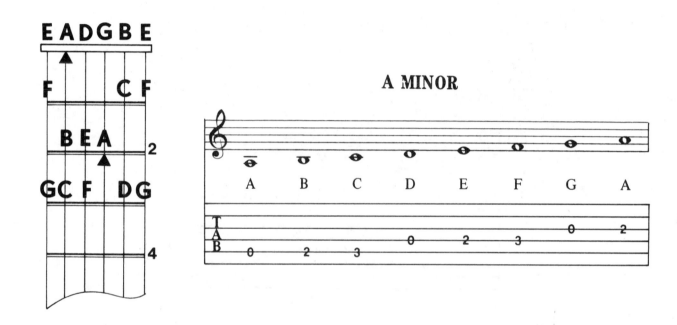

A MINOR

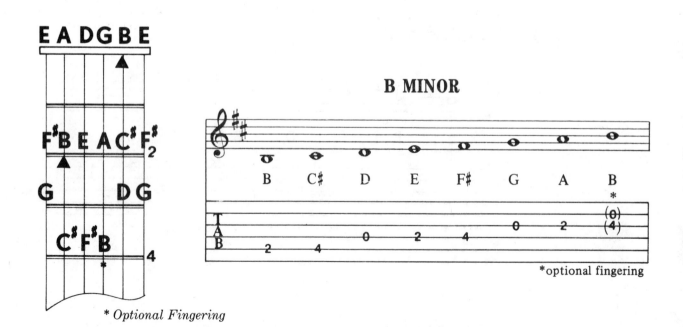

B MINOR

*optional fingering

* Optional Fingering

MINOR SCALES—OPEN POSITION

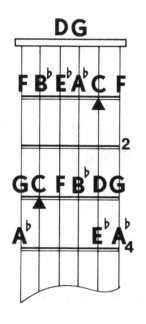

C MINOR

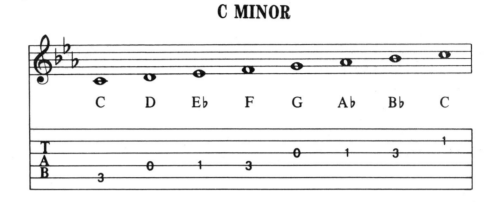

C D Eb F G Ab Bb C

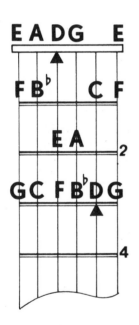

D MINOR

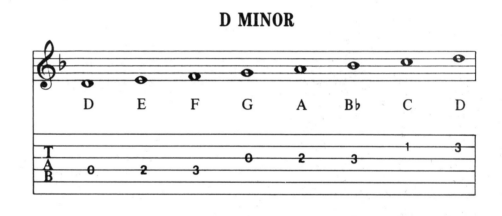

D E F G A Bb C D

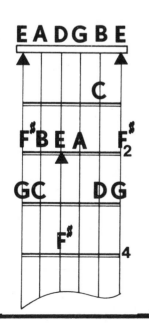

E MINOR

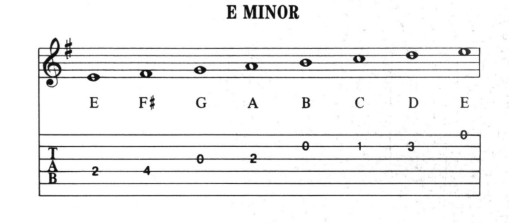

E F# G A B C D E

SCALES

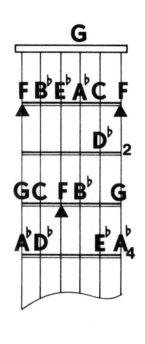

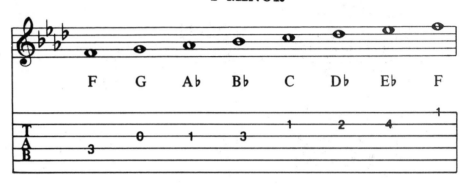

F MINOR

| F | G | Ab | Bb | C | Db | Eb | F |

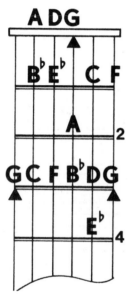

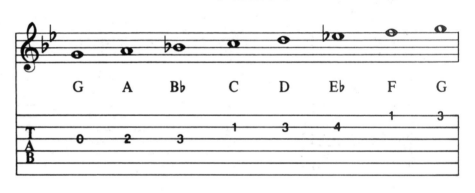

G MINOR

| G | A | Bb | C | D | Eb | F | G |

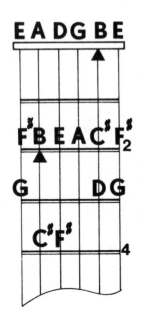

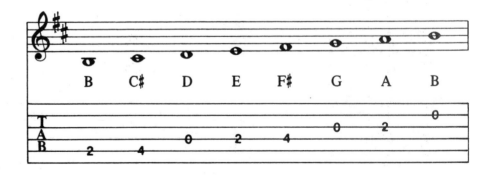

B MINOR

| B | C# | D | E | F# | G | A | B |

MINOR SCALES—OPEN POSITION

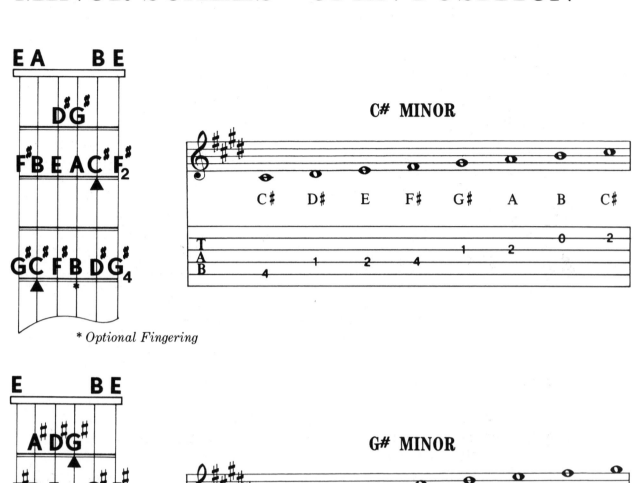

C# MINOR

*Optional Fingering

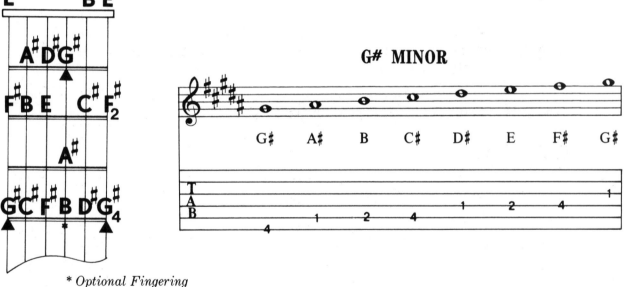

G# MINOR

*Optional Fingering

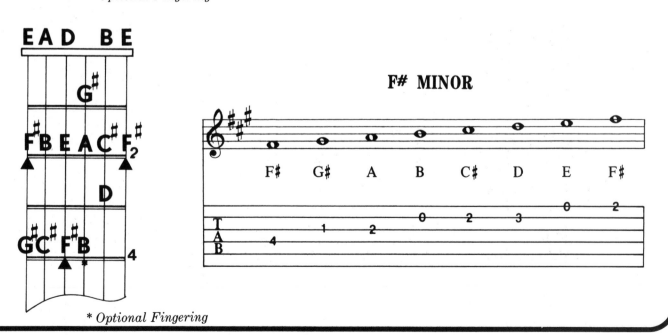

F# MINOR

*Optional Fingering

HARMONIC MINOR SCALE

In order to avoid the "minor" Dominant (V) chord that occurs when chord triads are built on the natural minor scale, the 7th note is raised a half-step to produce a Major Dominant (V) chord. This principle creates the HARMONIC MINOR SCALE. Using the harmonic minor scale — a step and a half between the 6th and 7th degrees (three frets apart on the guitar) — allows building PRIMARY CHORDS in a minor key to follow the rules of cadence.

The harmonic minor scale must be played over the Major Dominant (V) chord when improvising.

HARMONIC MINOR SCALE

HARMONIC MINOR SCALES

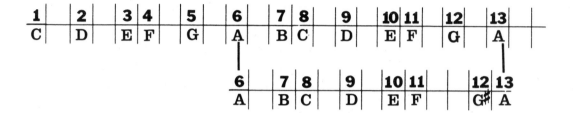

C MAJOR

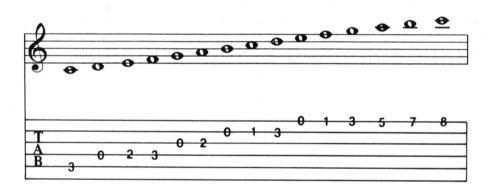

A harmonic minor

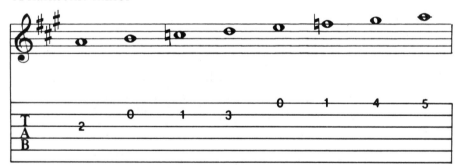

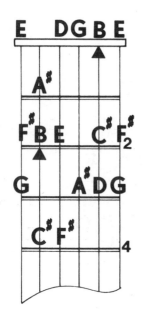

B HARMONIC MINOR

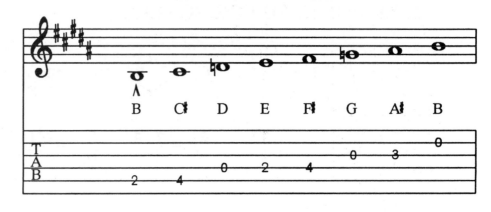

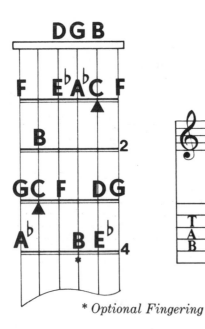

C HARMONIC MINOR

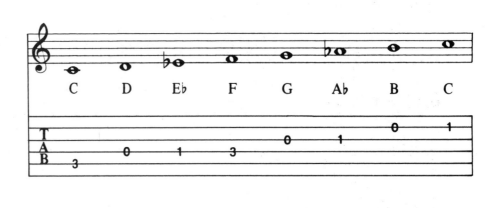

Optional Fingering

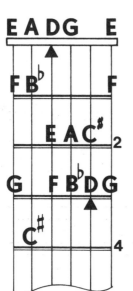

D HARMONIC MINOR

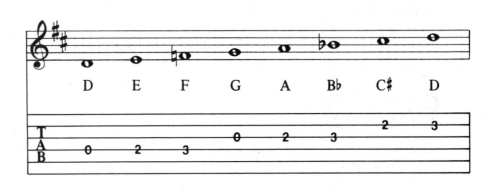

HARMONIC MINOR SCALE FORMS

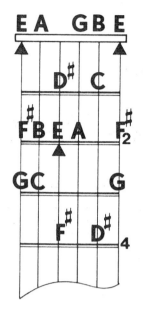

E HARMONIC MINOR

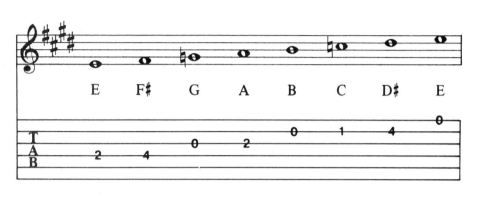

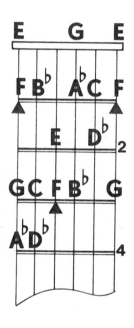

F HARMONIC MINOR

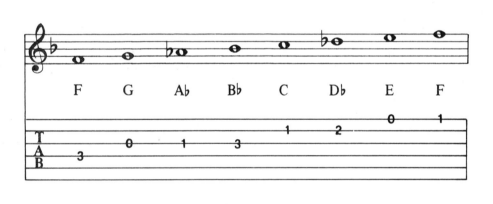

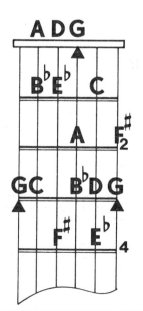

G HARMONIC MINOR

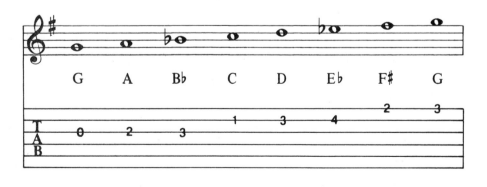

MELODIC MINOR SCALE

The Melodic Minor scale is comprised of two parts: the ascending movement with a half-step between the 7th and 8th notes, and a raised 6th note, which result in a smoother melodic "flow". The descending movement with the 6th and 7th notes lowered a half-step which produces the Natural Minor Scale.

The Melodic Minor scale is commonly called the JAZZ MINOR scale. This scale is formed by raising the 6th and 7th steps both ASCENDING and DECENDING.

MELODIC MINOR SCALES

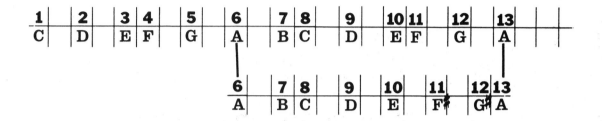

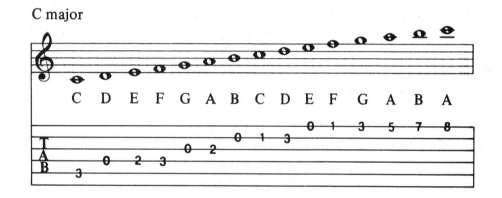

C major

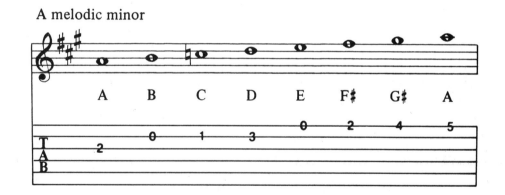

A melodic minor

SCALES

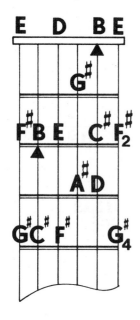

B MELODIC MINOR

B C# D E F# G# A# B

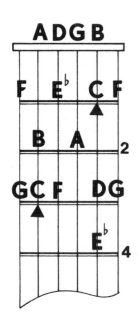

C MELODIC MINOR

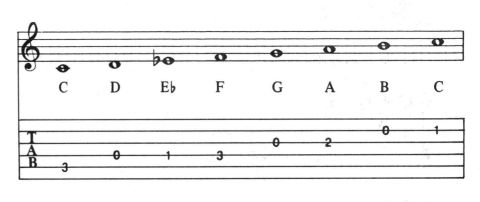

C D Eb F G A B C

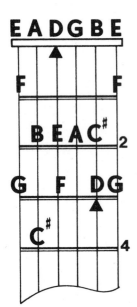

D MELODIC MINOR

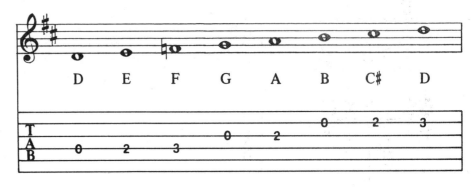

D E F G A B C# D

MELODIC MINOR SCALES

E MELODIC MINOR

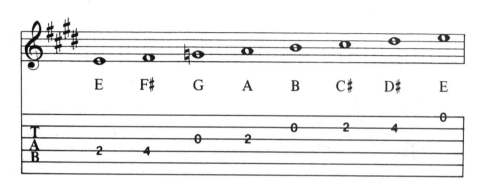

F MELODIC MINOR

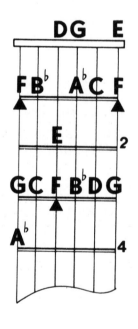

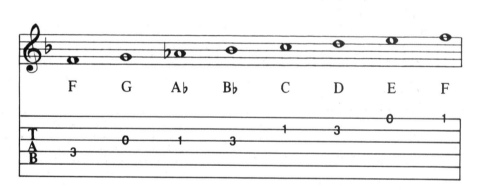

G MELODIC MINOR

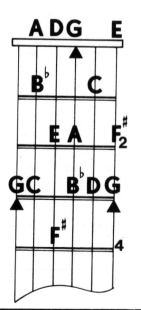

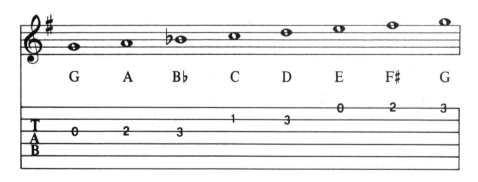

SCALES

PLAYING THE CLOSED POSITION

MAJOR SCALE FINGERING PATTERNS. As we have demonstrated, it is impractical to play scales in a linear movement (up and down the fingerboard). The "open position" can be most effective in creating many country, folk and bluegrass "licks". And, of course, it is the starting place for most beginners. The open position must be considered as a springboard to take you forward, a starting point upon which to build. It is the CLOSED POSITION that offers advantages unattainable either from the open position or linear movement. The advantages: Better note articulation, less chance of error, better continuity of tones, plus easy to comprehend "chord improvisation" capability.

The closed position patterns (scales, licks, runs) are movable fingering patterns — no open string tones. Each pattern moves chromatically, ascending or descending in pitch up or down the fingerboard without altering the pattern. The first note of the scale, the Tonic (Root) note, is the first note of the pattern.

THE CLOSED POSITION. We determine a CLOSED position by the location of the FIRST finger. If we place the first finger on the 2nd fret, we would be in the second position. The fingering for the THIRD position, as an example, would be as follows: First finger on the 3rd fret — it would also play notes on the second fret, a one fret stretch; second finger on the 4th fret; third finger on the 5th fret; fourth finger on the 6th fret — the fourth finger also is used to play notes on the 7th fret, a one fret stretch.

No open-string notes are utilized in closed position playing. Consequently, each position (each scale fingering pattern) is movable, and progresses chromatically. Since position playing allows movable patterns, each scale or pattern can be played in higher and lower positions on the fingerboard, allowing the guitarist to learn an arrangement in one key, and then easily change keys! The real importance of position playing will become clear as we study scale construction and finger positions.

There are many "movable scale positions", and only individual creativity limits how many we choose to use. Many patterns are of one octave and limited in usage, since most melodies extend well into two octaves. One-octave scale forms must be "connected" to other patterns, higher or lower on the fingerboard and are generally considered to be UP-AND-ACROSS scale patterns.

The TWO-OCTAVE movable scale position allows you to play in any key, for the sharps and flats of the key signature are of no concern because the pattern automatically generates all correct scale tones. An arrangement, once learned, may be transposed to any key within the range of the fingerboard that allows the complete position to be played.

Keep in mind that there is no singular way of presenting scale forms. The concepts presented in this book are solid, tried and provide required information to enhance your knowledge of music theory and the guitar fingerboard. It takes most guitarists years of playing and experimentation to develop a true working knowledge of solo and improvisational playing. Within the scope of this text, we present the more important and useful scale fingering patterns in the more commonly used positions.

It is not the intent of this text to teach "sight-reading". Neither is it prudent to include page after page of written scales, since this would be an exercise in sight-reading. Once fingering patterns have been committed to memory (note articulation and knowledge required of the individual scale mastered), you have learned the most important skills. The ability to "read" is a valuable educational asset and should be mastered. Sight-reading becomes a critical factor if you wish to continue your formal education and are required to read arrangements, or wish to put your music "on paper".

MOVABLE SCALE FORMS
Root on 6th String

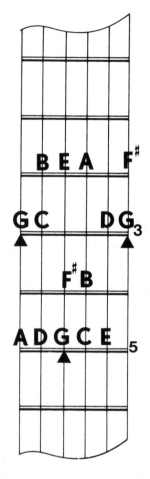

G MAJOR

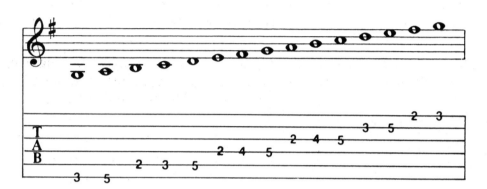

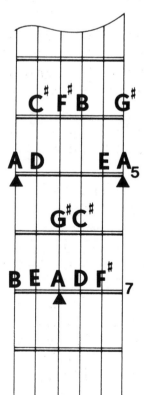

A MAJOR

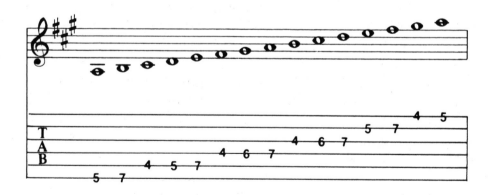

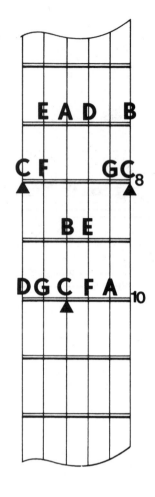

C MAJOR

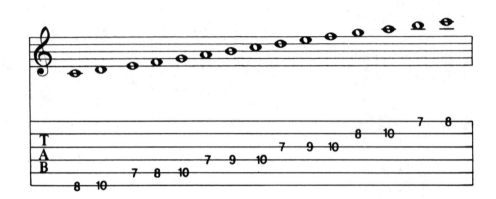

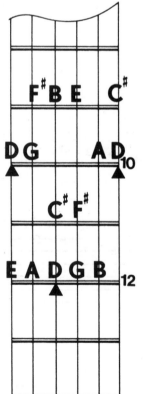

D MAJOR

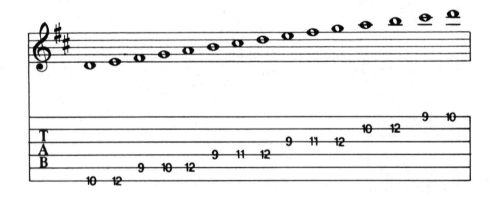

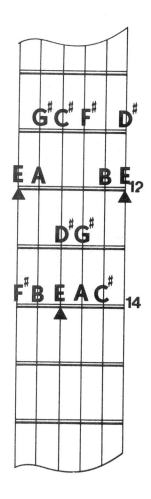

E MAJOR

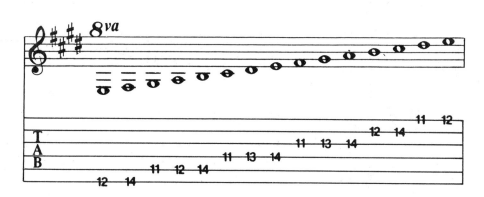

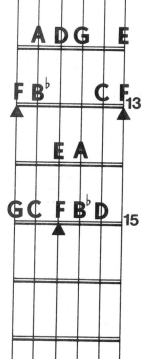

F MAJOR

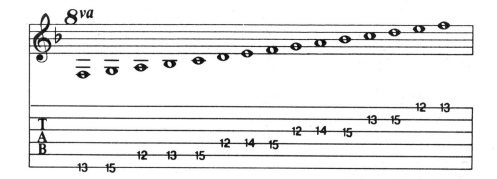

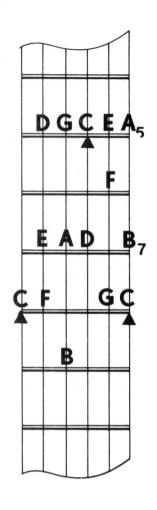

C MAJOR

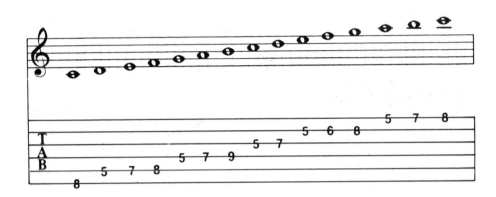

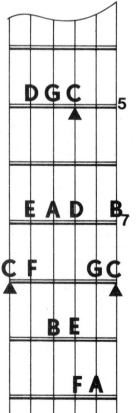

C MAJOR

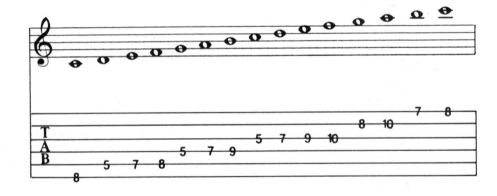

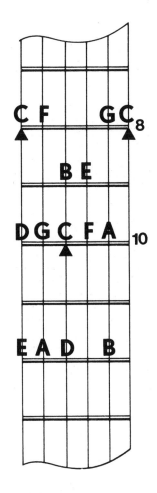

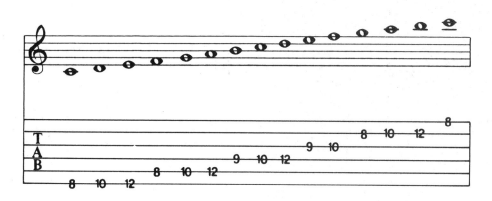

C MAJOR

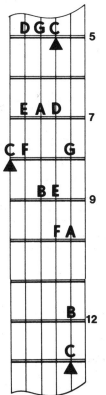

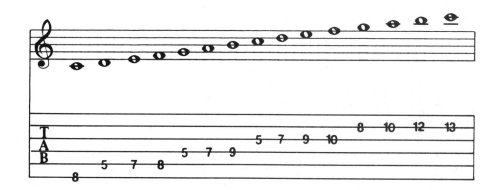

C MAJOR

ONE OCTAVE MOVABLE SCALE FORM
(Root Note on the 5th String)

There are many combinations of note patterns capable of creating scales, and it is desirable to know as many scale patterns as possible. Within the scope of this book, the fingering shapes and forms are presented that guitarists use most often. Once you fully understand the concepts presented, try finding other scale patterns — new ways of moving about the fingerboard.

ROOT NOTE ON THE 5TH STRING. The tonic note follows the chromatic scale on the 5th string.

These two-octave scale patterns commence on the 5th string. It will require extensive practice to become comfortable with this position, since the left hand must "arch" over the fingerboard to allow good four-finger articulation. Remember, make each finger responsible for one fret.

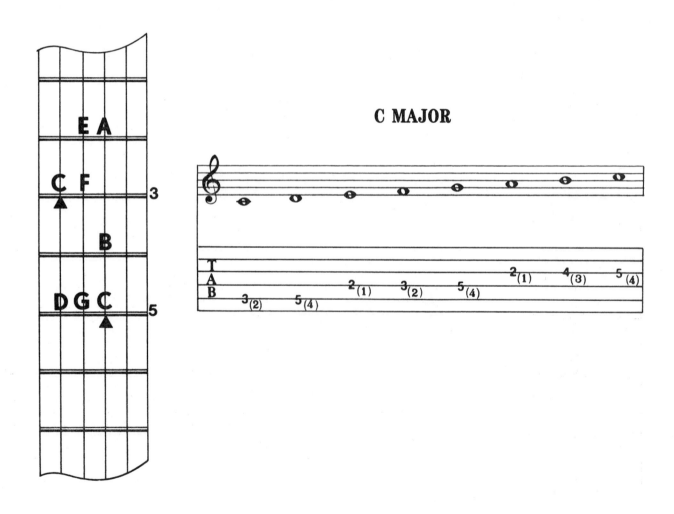

C MAJOR

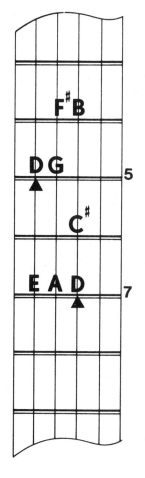

D MAJOR

D major

D E F# G A B C# D

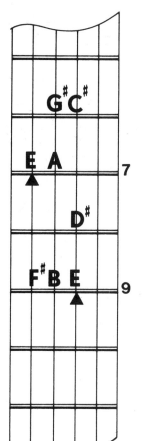

E MAJOR

E major

E F# G# A B C# D# E

ROOT NOTE ON THE 3RD STRING

Another one-octave scale, Tonic (Root) note, follows the chromatic scale of the 3rd string, ascending or descending in pitch. It is worth practicing this scale pattern at every fret, training the fingers to compensate for the variations in the spacing of the frets. Playing the guitar is a combination of mental and motor skills.

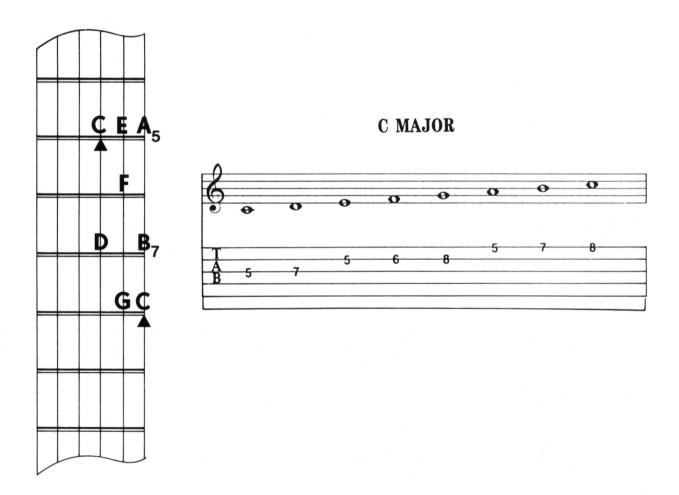

C MAJOR

MOVABLE SCALE FORMS
Root on 3th String

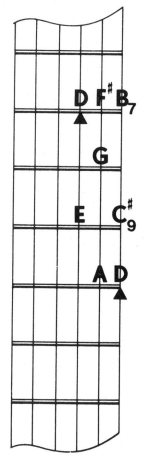

D major

D MAJOR

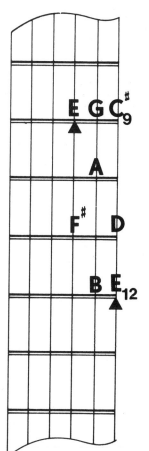

E major

E MAJOR

TWO-OCTAVE "UP AND ACROSS" MAJOR SCALE PATTERNS

This is a two-octave pattern with the root note on the 5th string. To play the second octave requires a one fret "shift". The first finger must move up one fret to play the first note of the second octave. The first finger also plays the first note on the 1st string. Be sure to "walk" the note pattern on the 1st string. The fourth finger should play the last note. Executed properly, this is an efficient and easy scale pattern to play in ascending order. The descending movement, as with many scale patterns, does not flow as smoothly and will require practice.

"UP-and-ACROSS" PATTERNS

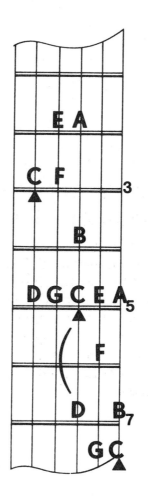

C MAJOR

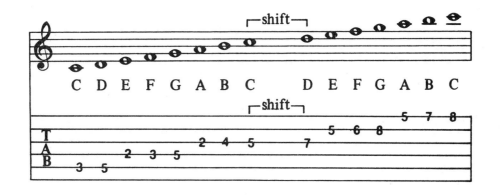

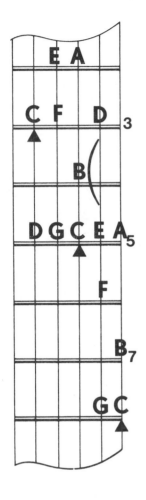

C MAJOR

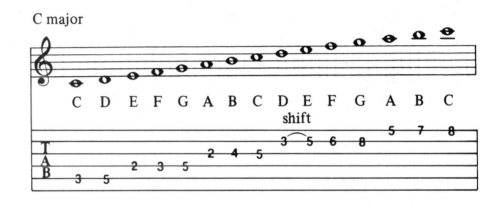

C MAJOR

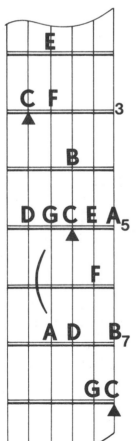

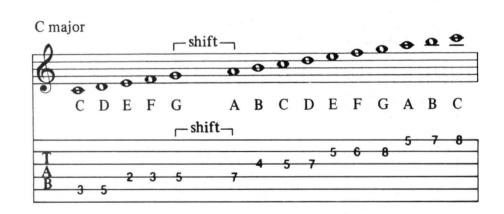

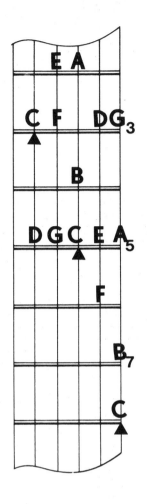

C MAJOR

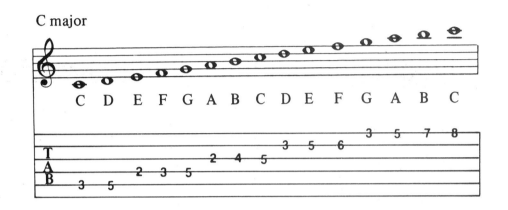

C MAJOR

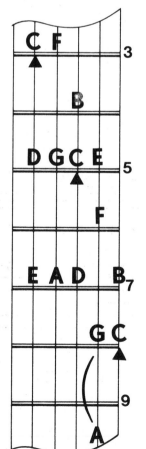

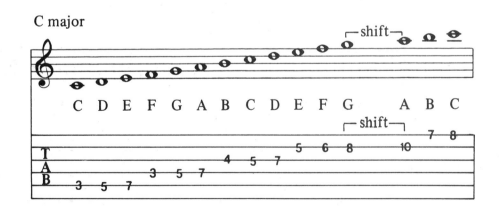

These Natural Minor scale forms are all movable fingering patterns. Each pattern moves chromatically up and down the fingerboard. The first note of the scale, the Tonic or Root note, is the first note of the pattern (marked with a black check mark). These fingering patterns produce all correct notes — sharps and flats included. Practice these patterns until they feel comfortable.

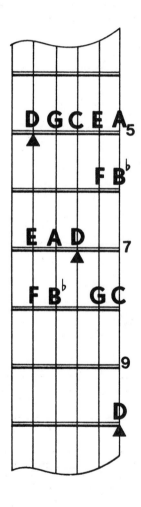

D NATURAL MINOR

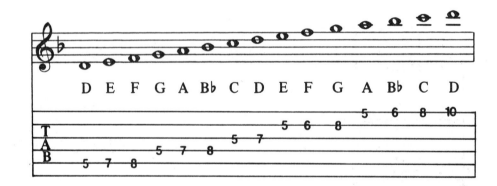

NATURAL MINOR SCALE FORMS

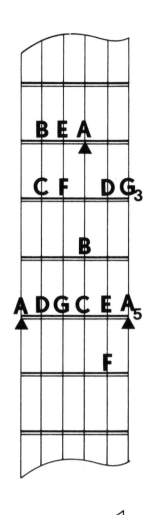

A NATURAL MINOR

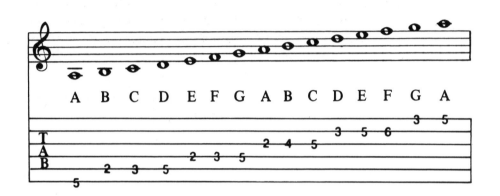

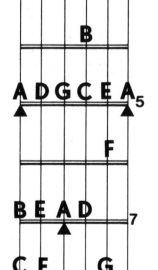

A NATURAL MINOR

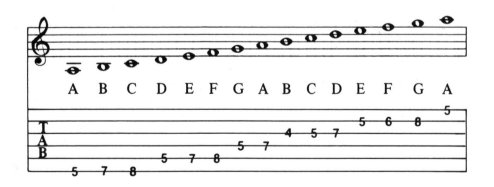

These Melodic Minor scale forms are all movable fingering patterns. Each pattern moves chromatically up and down the fingerboard. The first note of the scale, the Tonic or Root note, is the first note of the pattern (marked with a black check mark). These fingering patterns produce all correct notes — sharps and flats included. Practice these patterns until they feel comfortable.

The "movable" harmonic minor scale forms contain no open strings and moves chromatically, ascending and descending in pitch with the Root fingering position naming the scale played.

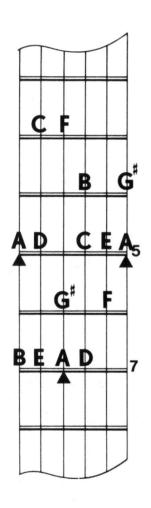

A HARMONIC MINOR

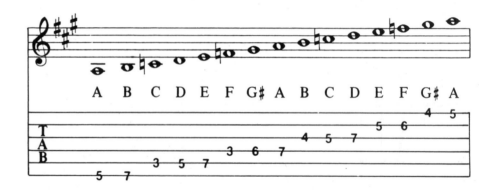

A B C D E F G# A B C D E F G# A

HARMONIC-MELODIC MINORS
SCALE FORMS

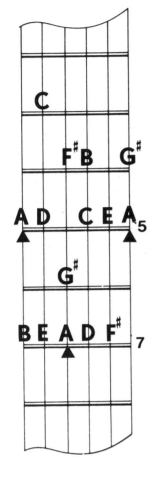

A MELODIC MINOR — Ascending

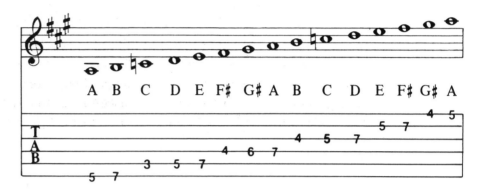

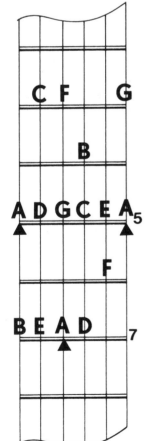

A MELODIC MINOR — Descending (A natural minor)

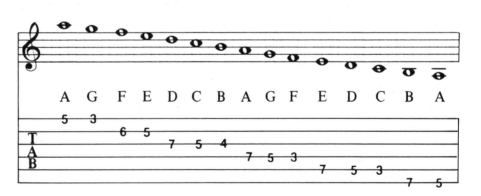

SCALES

MOVABLE CHORDS AND THE
POSITION SCALE RELATIONSHIP

In any key, there are three chords which appear in virtually every basic progression. They will always sound good together, in whatever order they are played. They are called the PRIMARY CHORDS. They are chords built on the TONIC (I), SUB-DOMINANT (IV) and DOMINANT (V) degrees of the scale. In any key, these three chords have the same relationship to one another. The two-octave scale position contains all notes required to build the triads of these three chords. Example: In the key of *G* Major, the TONIC chord is *G*, chord tones — *G B D;* the SUB-DOMINANT chord is *C*, chord tones — *C E G;* the DOMINANT chord is *D*, chord tones — *D F♯ A.*

By playing the BARRE CHORDS (no open strings), it is possible to interlock the primary chords with the two-octave scale position. By knowing how to play the two-octave scale position and the three Barre Chord forms, you can play lead or rhythm from a fixed position, in any key.

Barre chords are movable forms. The same shape can be moved up and down the fingerboard without altering the fingering, the first finger replaces the nut of the guitar, thus each barre chord form may be played anywhere on the fingerboard. Like movable scale forms, they move chromatically. Each chord form produces twelve chords; one for each note of the chromatic scale.

In most common usage there are three barre chord forms. They are, in their lowest playing position, where the NUT replaces the first finger barre, the FORM ONE, open string *E* major chord; FORM TWO, open string *A* chord; and FORM THREE, the open string *C* chord. These three chord forms become the three primary chords of the key and are within the note pattern of the two-octave scale position.

NOTE: To achieve a PERFECT CADENCE, dominant chords are played as DOMINANT SEVENTH chords. The form three barre chord may be played as a dominant seventh. However, the fingering reduces the chord to four strings.

MOVABLE SCALES-MOVABLE CHORDS

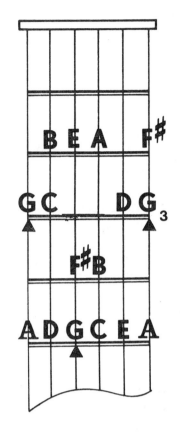

G MAJOR

1		2		3	4		5		6		7	8
G		A		B	C		D		E		F#	G

THREE PRIMARY CHORD-KEY OF G MAJOR

FORM 1	FORM 2	FORM 3
G MAJOR	**C** MAJOR	**D** MAJOR

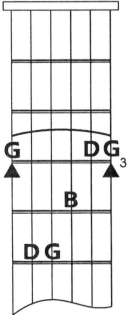
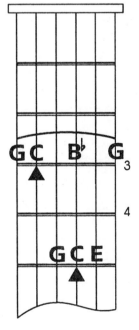
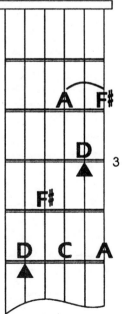

MODES

MODES
MODES
MODES
MODES
MODES
MODES
MODES
MODES
MODES
MODES
MODES
MODES
MODES
MODES
MODES
MODES
MODES
MODES
MODES
MODES
MODES

MODES

THE ORIGINS OF MODES

(Illustration One) "Ionian, Dorian, Phrygian, Lydian, Mixoldian, Aeolian, Locrian, my word!", the student exclaimed in confusion, "It's all Greek to me!" And so it is. We often blame the Greeks for ideas and words we fail to comprehend. However, our modern concept of "structured" music is Greek in origin, and the seven scales accredited to them are named after seven of their most important tribes.

In the fifteenth and sixteenth centuries, musicians within the Christian Church began using these ancient scales. However, they introduced various changes. Originally, the scales were played in DESCENDING order. This was changed so the scales ASCENDED. These "modern" musicians changed the note from which the scale began, and they substituted the term MODE for SCALE. This new structure meant that the Greek Dorian Scale, in the key of *C* Major, became the Dorian Modes and went up from *D* to *D;* the Phrygian Mode ascended from *E* to *E,* and Mixolydian Mode went up from *G* to *G.* The Greek Lydian Scale, which originally descended from *C,* now ascended from *C* and was renamed the Ionian Mode. The scale that began on the note *A* was now called the Aeolian Mode.

Many of these Medieval Folk scales and Chordal works are being reintroduced. We find these scale forms commonly used in modern Jazz, Blues and Folk arrangements.

A MODE is an INVERSION of a Major Scale, a variation, where one of the notes of the scale other than the tonic serves as the Root of the Mode. Example: *(Illustration One)* In the Key of *C* Major, we might begin on the sixth degree (note *A*), and play through the *C* Major scale, *A* to *A,* the Aeolian Mode. Each mode covers the range of a chromatic scale, and like the Diatonic Major Scale, steps through the thirteen-note octave. However, the step, half-step pattern particular to each mode produces a different series of scale tones.

ILLUSTRATION ONE

MODAL TERMINOLOGY

C MAJOR

Ionian	Dorian	Phrygian	Lydian	Mixolydian	Aeolian	Locrian	Ionian
I	II	III	IV	V	VI	VII	VIII

ILLUSTRATION TWO

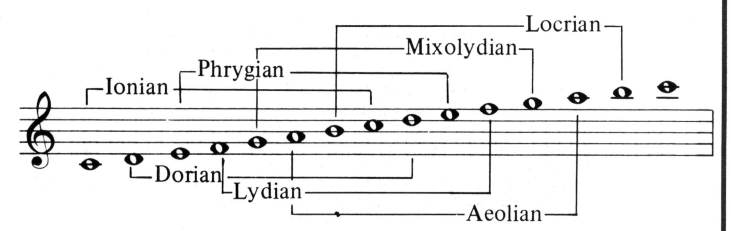

WORKING OUT MODES

Modes are scales created through the displacement of the major scale and are usually taught as a DERIVATIVE of the "parent" scale.

The DORIAN MODE in the key of *G* Major, is a scale starting on the second degree — note *A*, and continuing through the *G* scale: *A B C D E F# G A.*

Thinking of a mode as a derivative of a major scale is quite easy — if you know how to play movable major scales and can name each note played. In the key of *E* Major *(Illustration Two)*, what is the name of the third scale note? *(G#)*. A mode built on the third note of a major scale is called the PHRYGIAN MODE (third mode), and by playing the *E* Major scale from the third note would create the *G#* Phrygian mode.

Since these modes are a derivative of the parent scale (same fingering pattern), it is not necessary to worry about the correct placement of the half-steps required to produce each mode. The sound characteristic of each mode can be translated into any key so long as its original step, half-step pattern is not altered.

WORKING OUT MODES

ILLUSTRATION ONE

A DORIAN MODE

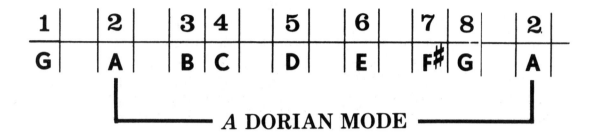

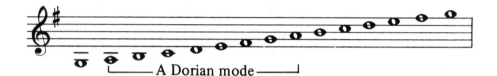

ILLUSTRATION TWO

G# PHRYGIAN MODE

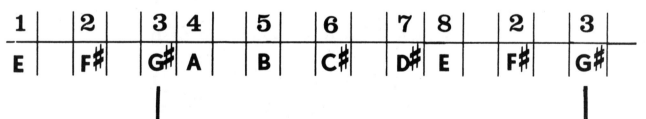

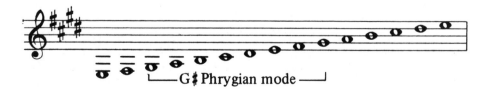

MODES

DERIVATIVE MODES
(In the Key of C Major)

At first, the untrained ear will have trouble accepting the dissonance associated with the placement of mode half-steps. However, it is important to realize that is is this location of the half-steps that provides the individual tonal characteristics of each mode.

The formula for building modes (the step, half-step pattern of each mode) produces five new scales, not seven. Since the Ionian Mode built on the first degree and the Aeolian Mode built on the sixth degrees are the same as the Major Diatonic and Natural Minor Scales. These five new scales represent an alternative to the melodic and harmonic structures of the diatonic scale.

The Ionian (*I-O-NE-AN*) Mode

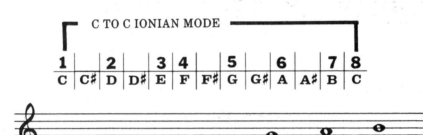

The Dorian (*DOR-E-AN*) Mode

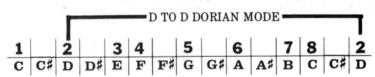

The Phrygian (*FRIG-E-AN*) Mode

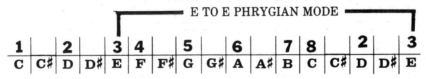

DERIVATIVE MODES

The Lydian (*LID-E-AN*) Mode

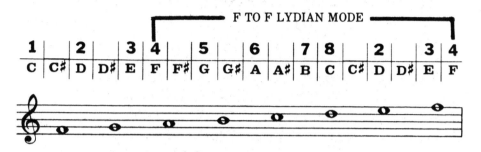

The Mixolydian (*MIX-O-LID-E-AN*) Mode

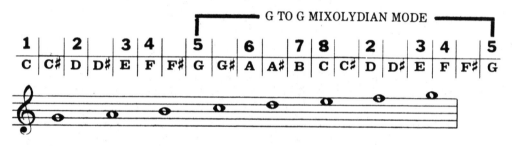

The Aeolian (*E-O-LE-AN*) Mode

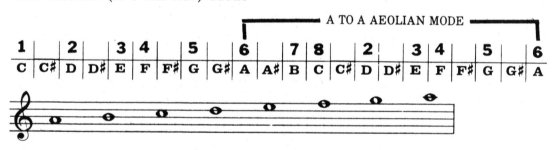

The Locrian (*LO-CRI-AN*) Mode

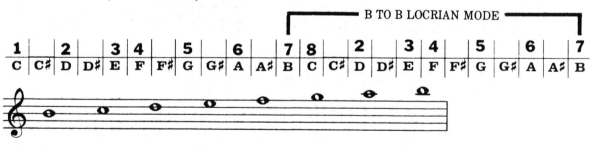

PLAYING DERIVATIVE MODES
FROM MOVABLE SCALE FORMS

Modes, when played from a "movable" scale form, ascend and descend chromatically. *Illustration One* presents one form. The Root note appears on the 6th string, while the octave note is on the 3rd string and appears again on the 1st string.

Illustration Two shows another movable scale. This form (the Phrygian mode) starts on the 5th string with the octave on the 3rd string. A "shift" is required to play the complete pattern — octave note (*E*), is on the twelfth fret, first string.

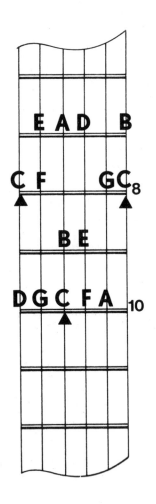

C MAJOR IONIAN MODE (C Ionian)

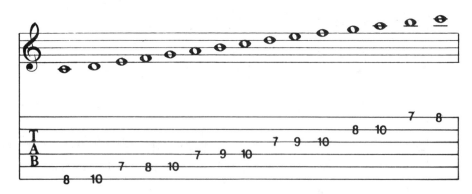

HOW TO FIND A DERIVATIVE MODAL SCALE

Remember: Dorian is the name given to a mode that commences on the second degree (note) of a major scale.

Question: To play the *A* Dorian mode, what major scale is the note *A*, the second degree?

Answer: The note *A* is the second degree of the *G* Major scale.,

Remember: Lydian is the mode built on the fourth degree of a major scale.

Question: To play the *E* Lydian mode, which major scale is the note *E* the fourth degree?

Answer: The note *E* is the fourth degree of *B* major. Play the *B* major scale from *E* to *E*.

DERIVATIVE MODES FROM MOVABLE CHORD FORMS

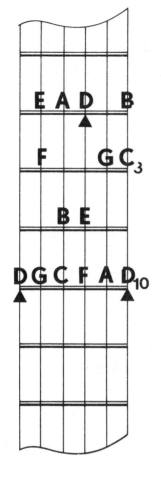

ILLUSTRATION ONE

C MAJOR DORIAN MODE (D Dorian)

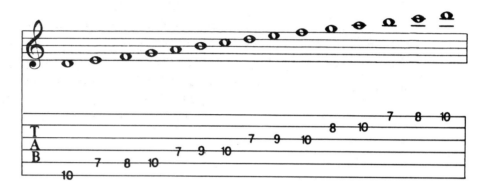

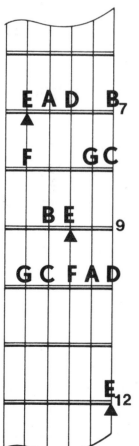

ILLUSTRATION TWO

C MAJOR PHRYGIAN MODE (E Phrygian)

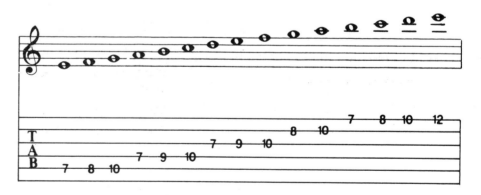

MODES

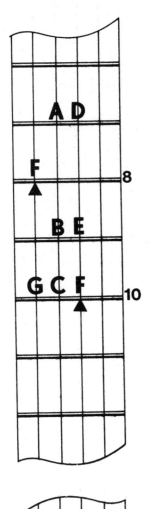

C MAJOR LYDIAN MODE (F Lydian)

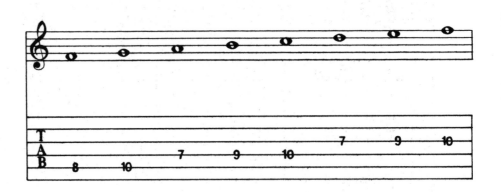

C MAJOR MIXOLYDIAN MODE (G Mixolydian)

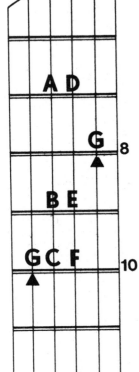

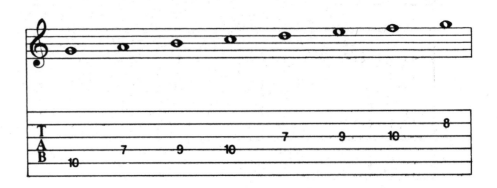

DERIVATIVE MODES FROM MOVABLE CHORD FORMS

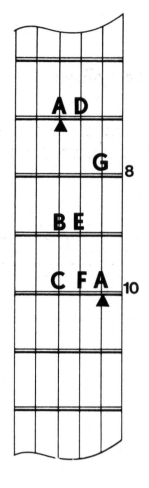

C MAJOR AEOLIAN MODE (A Aeolian)

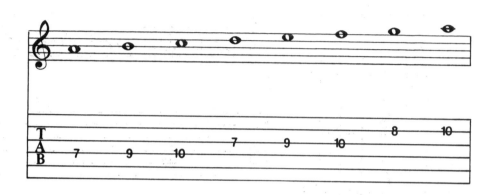

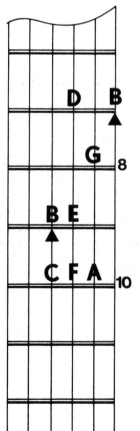

C MAJOR LOCRIAN MODE (B Locrian)

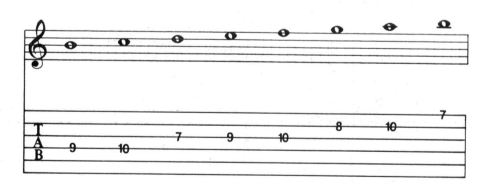

MODES

PARALLEL MODES

Our approach, up to this point, has been derivative — each mode derived from the major scale, played from the same root note (*C* Major in most examples). This approach to modal playing contains advantages as well as certain disadvantages. The derivative approach relies upon your knowledge and mastery of a few six-string movable scale forms. A more comprehensive understanding of modes is possible by comparing modes in PARALLEL with the parent major scale. In the beginning, the parallel approach is more complex. You must know the correct step, half-step pattern of each mode. Consequently, your knowledge of the fingerboard will be tested.

DERIVATIVE. The DORIAN mode in the Key of *C* Major is a scale starting on the second degree — note *D: D E F G A B C D*, the *D* Dorian mode.

PARALLEL. The Dorian mode is a *D* Major scale played with a lowered 3rd and a lowered 7th: *D E F G A B C D*.

Free improvisation usually works well from a derivative approach. However, if required to sight-read an arrangement and quickly play a modal scale over a written chord symbol, derivative thinking might be too slow. For instance, if the chord symbol is *Bb* Lydian, what approach is quickest? The parallel approach: What major scale is *Bb* the fourth degree? The derivative approach: Build a Lydian scale, the *Bb* Major scale with a raised fourth. In this situation, parallel thinking is quicker than derivative.

MODE APPLICATIONS . . . SUBSTATIONS

CHORD TYPES	MODES(S)
Major 7th	Ionian; Lydian; Lydian #2; Lydian Augmented
Minor 7th	Dorian; Phrygian; Aeolian; Dorian # 4
Minor 7 b5	Locrian
Dominant 7th	Mixolydian; Lydian b7; Aeolian Major; Phrygian Major; Dorian b2
Major 7 # 5	Lydian Augmented

HARMONIZATION OF MODES

DORIAN MODE. The Dorian mode plays through the following chords: Minor 7th, minor 9th, 13ths, and minor 6/9.

THE PHRYGIAN MODE. The Phrygian mode generates the minor 7th and minor 9th chords.

THE LYDIAN MODE. The Lydian mode plays well over major chords; major 7th; major 9th, major #11th. With an added flat 7th, it may be used over Dominant 7th chords.

THE MIXOLYDIAN MODE. The Mixolydian mode is formed by flatting the 7th note of a major scale. It may be played over unaltered dominant chords (*C7, C9, C11, C13*). Altered Dominant chords would, for example, have a flat 15th, augmented 9th, etc.

THE AEOLIAN MODE. The Aeolian mode may be played over minor 7th, minor 9th, minor 11th and minor 13th chords.

THE LOCRIAN MODE. The Locrian mode plays well over the minor 7 b5 chord.

PARALLEL MODES

IONIAN

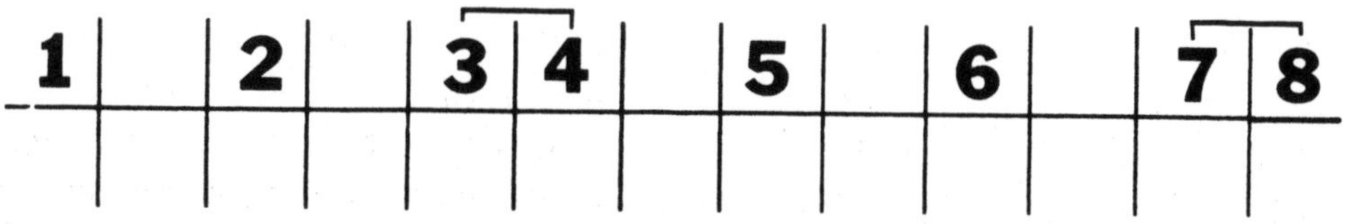

| 1 | 2 | 3 4 | 5 | 6 | 7 8 |

DORIAN

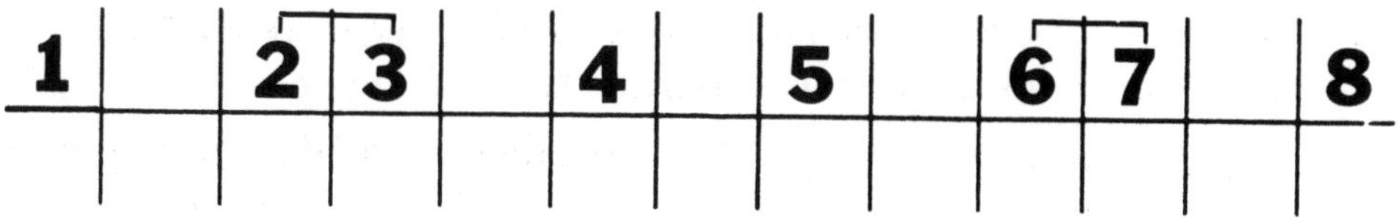

| 1 | 2 3 | 4 | 5 | 6 7 | 8 |

PHRYGIAN

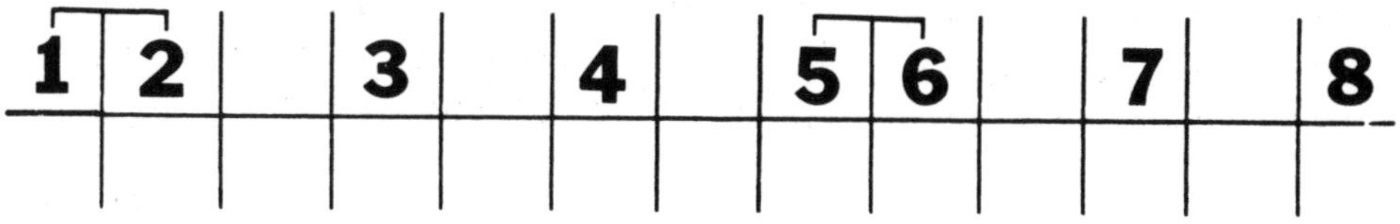

| 1 2 | 3 | 4 | 5 6 | 7 | 8 |

LYDIAN

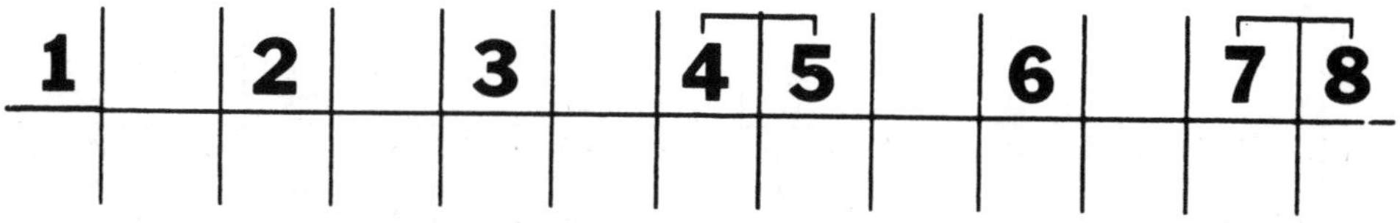

| 1 | 2 | 3 | 4 5 | 6 | 7 8 |

MIXOLYDIAN

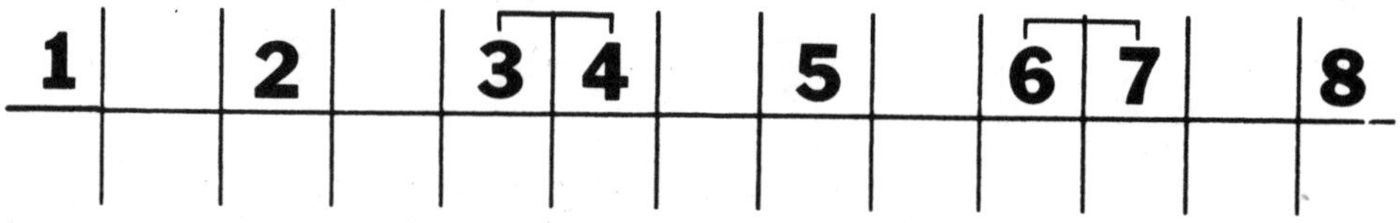

| 1 | 2 | 3 4 | 5 | 6 7 | 8 |

AEOLIAN

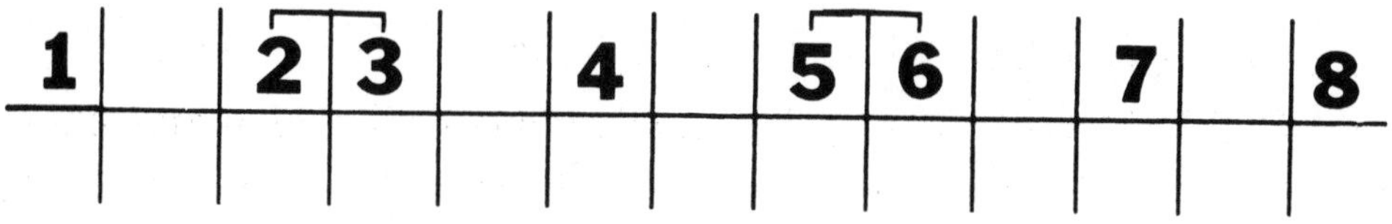

| 1 | 2 3 | 4 | 5 6 | 7 | 8 |

LOCRIAN

| 1 2 | 3 | 4 5 | 6 | 7 | 8 |

These Parallel Mode scale forms are all movable fingering patterns. Each pattern moves chromatically up and down the fingerboard. The first note of the scale, the Tonic or Root note, is the first note of the pattern (marked with a black check mark). These fingering patterns produce all correct notes — sharps and flats included. Practice these patterns until they feel comfortable.

C IONIAN MODE (Same as Major scale)

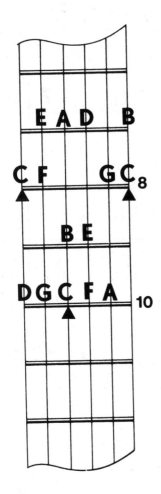

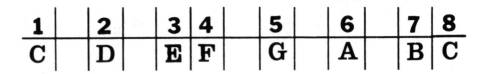

1	2	3	4	5	6	7	8
C	D	E	F	G	A	B	C

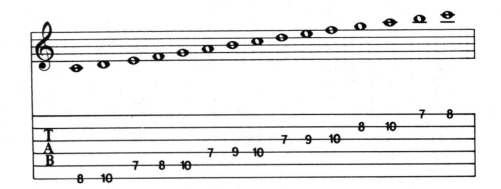

PARALLEL MODES FROM MOVABLE SCALE FORMS

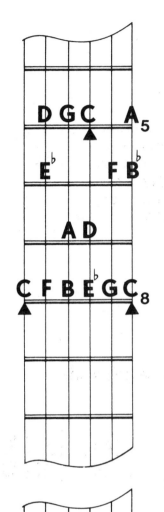

C DORIAN MODE

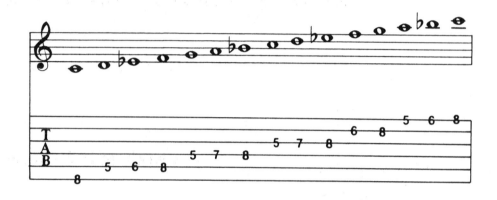

1		2	3		4		5		6	7		8
C		D	E♭		F		G		A	B♭		C

C PHRYGIAN MODE

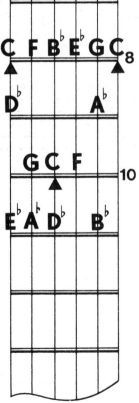

1	2		3		4		5	6		7		8
C	D♭		E♭		F		G	A♭		B♭		C

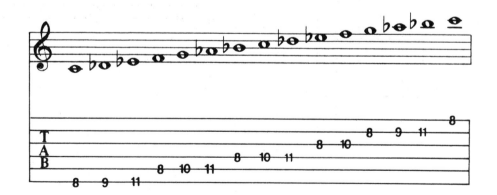

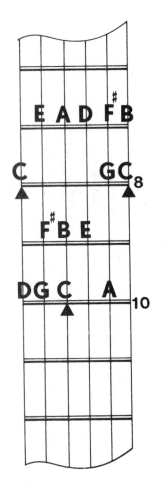

C LYDIAN MODE

1	2	3	4	5	6	7	8
C	D	E	F♯	G	A	B	C

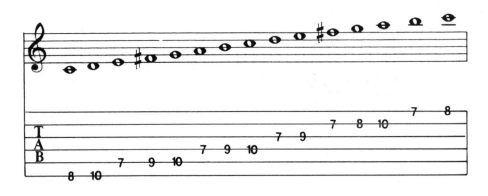

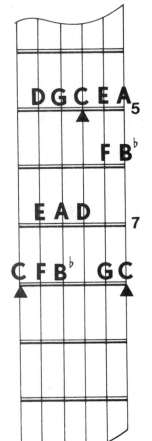

C MIXOLYDIAN MODE

1	2	3	4	5	6	7	8
C	D	E	F	G	A	B♭	C

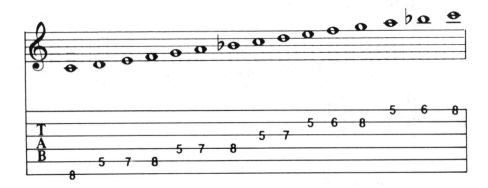

PARALLEL MODES FROM MOVABLE SCALE FORMS

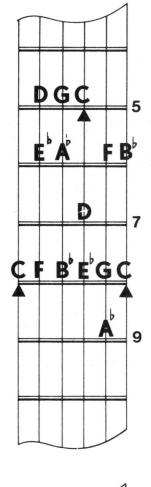

C AEOLIAN MODE

1	2	3	4	5	6	7	8
C	D	E♭	F	G	A♭	B♭	C

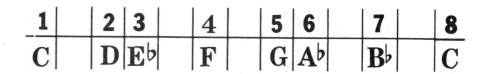

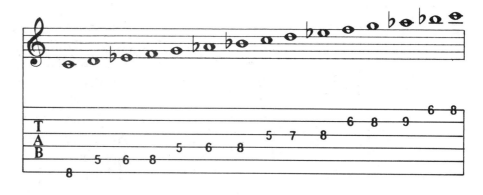

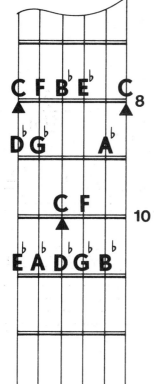

C LOCRIAN MODE

1	2	3	4	5	6	7	8
C	D♭	E♭	F	G♭	A♭	B♭	C

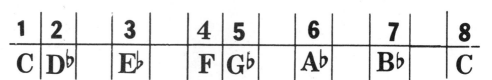

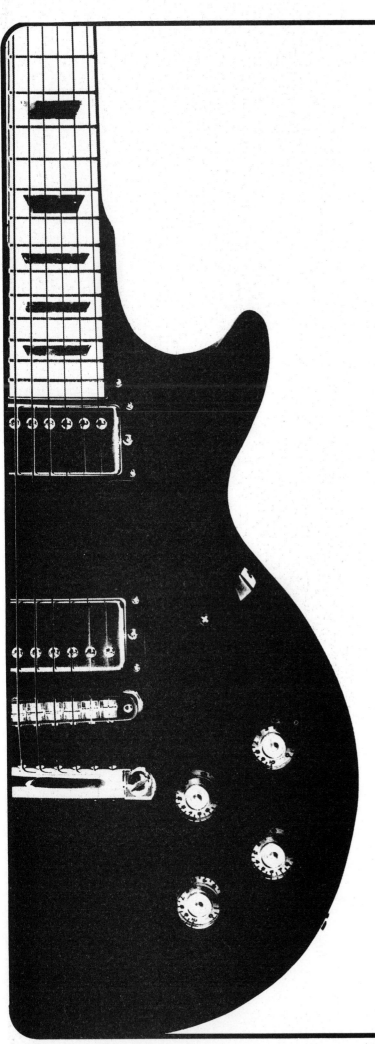

ALTERED SCALES

ALTERED SCALES
ALTERED SCALES
ALTERED SCALES
ALTERED SCALES
ALTERED SCALES
ALTERED SCALES
ALTERED SCALES
ALTERED SCALES
ALTERED SCALES
ALTERED SCALES
ALTERED SCALES
ALTERED SCALES
ALTERED SCALES
ALTERED SCALES
ALTERED SCALES
ALTERED SCALES
ALTERED SCALES
ALTERED SCALES
ALTERED SCALES
ALTERED SCALES
ALTERED SCALES
ALTERED SCALES

PENTATONIC SCALES

PENTATONIC is derived from the Latin word "PENTA" (meaning five). Pentatonic scales are FIVE note scales. They are one of the oldest and most widespread scales in common usage. They are thought to have Mongolian and Japanese origins.

There are two types of commonly used five-note Pentatonic Scales: Major and Minor. A third scale, an ALTERED Pentatonic (or six-note Blues scale), completes this popular group of improvisational scale forms.

The Major Pentatonic Scale is a select pattern of major scale notes — a major scale with the 4th and 7th degrees left out, and may be used interchangeable with the Major Scale of the same key signature.

The Major Pentatonic Scale (no 7th) may be played over Dominant chords, chords with a lowered seventh (13th 5b7), and works equally well against Major Seventh chords, chords with a natural seventh (1357). The Major Pentatonic Scale emphasizes the 6th and 9th degrees, and creates the traditional "sweet-country" sound.

The guitar, tuned to "standard pitch" ($E\ A\ D\ G\ B\ E$), is an expanded G MAJOR PENTATONIC SCALE.

The PENTATONIC MINOR scale is a five-note scale with a Minor Third. It is a NATURAL MINOR scale with the 2nd and 6th degree left out. The Pentatonic Minor scale may be substituted for a Melodic Minor scale.

The BLUES scale is a Pentatonic Minor scale with a raised 4th degree. This one additional note adds an interesting "Bluesy" sound and is used extensively in Rock, Blues and Jazz improvisation.

These two Pentatonic scales and the Blues scales share the same chordal relationship as diatonic major and minor scales. They may be played over an entire chord progression — it is not necessary to change scales when the chord changes.

When played from a CLOSED POSITION, these scales, like the major scale forms, move chromatically.

PENTATONIC SCALES

PENTATONIC MAJOR 5 NOTE "Country" Scale

1	2	3		4	5		6
C	D	E		G	A		C

PENTATONIC MINOR 5 NOTE "Blues" Scale

1		2	3	4		5	6
C		E♭	F	G		B♭	C

PENTATONIC MINOR 6 NOTE "Blues" Scale

1		2	3	4	5		6	7
C		E♭	F	F♯	G		B♭	C

G MAJOR PENTATONIC SCALE

(Open strings-standard tuning)

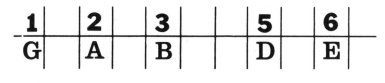

1	2	3		5	6
G	A	B		D	E

strings   5TH   3RD   4TH   1ST

These Pentatonic Minor scale forms are all movable fingering patterns. Each pattern moves chromatically up and down the fingerboard. The first note of the scale, the Tonic or Root note, is the first note of the pattern (marked with a black check mark). These fingering patterns produce all correct notes — sharps and flats included. Practice these patterns until they feel comfortable.

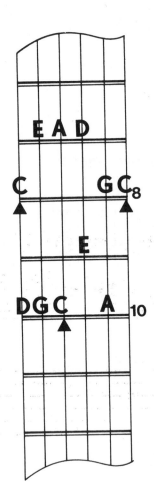

PENTATONIC MINOR (5 note 'blues scale')

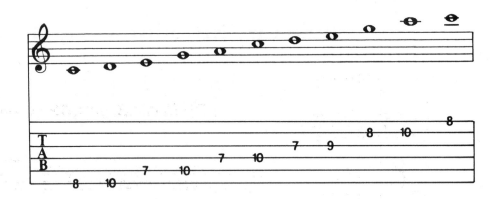

PENTATONIC SCALES-MOVABLE FORMS

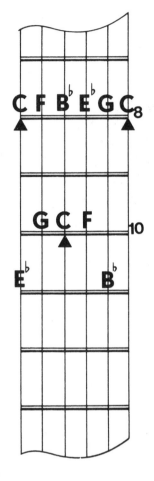

PENTATONIC MINOR (5 note 'blues scale')

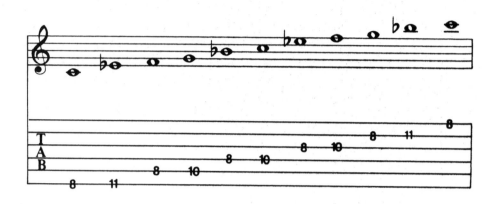

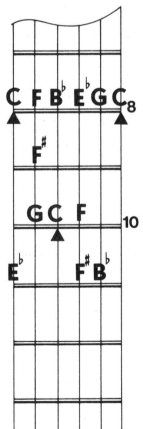

PENTATONIC MINOR (6 note 'blues scale')

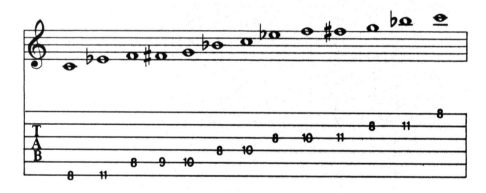

THE WHOLE-TONE SCALE

The WHOLE-TONE scale divides the octave into six equal intervals (whole steps). It has a "floating" tonal characteristic without a strong, specific key *C* center. There are no half-steps, and with the absence of these semi-tones, the scale sounds the same from whatever note you start.

Only TWO whole-tone scales are required in order to play all twelve keys, one starts on the note *C* and the other on *C#*. The first note played names the scale.

The whole-tone scale is also called an AUGMENTED scale. This scale is a useful compositional form and allows harmonic possibilities not possible with the diatonic scale.

The whole-tone scale may be played over Dominant 7 #5 and Dominant 9 #5 chords.

ILLUSTRATION ONE

C MAJOR WHOLE-TONE SCALE

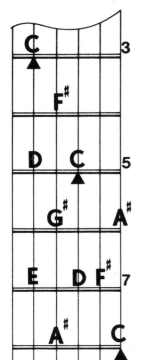

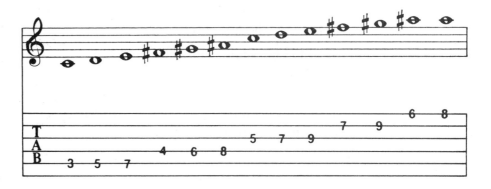

ILLUSTRATION TWO

C# WHOLE-TONE SCALE

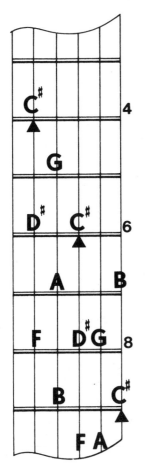

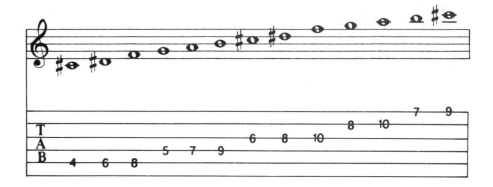

THE DIMINISHED SCALE

The DIMINISHED scale divides the octave into eight intervals and contains nine notes. The interval placement is a series of step, half-step patterns. Each diminished scale has four key-centers. The diminished scale formulation of step, half-step, produces only THREE diminished scales that include all twelve keys. One starts on *C*, the second on *C#/Db*, and the third starts on *D*.

The *C* diminished scale (*C D Eb F Gb Ab A B*) contains the same notes as the *Eb*, *Gb* and *A* diminished scales. *C#* diminished

D diminished scale contains the same notes as *F*, *Ab* and *B* diminished scales.

Melodies and chords built on diminished scales are very unlike melodies built on diatonic scales. Diminished scales, like Whole-Tone scales, suggest more than one key-center.

C DIMINISHED SCALE

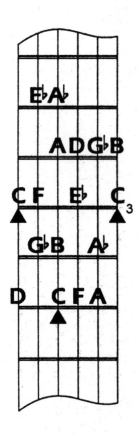

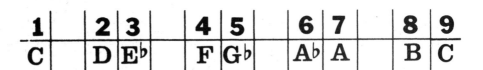

1		2	3		4	5		6	7		8	9
C		D	E♭		F	G♭		A♭	A		B	C

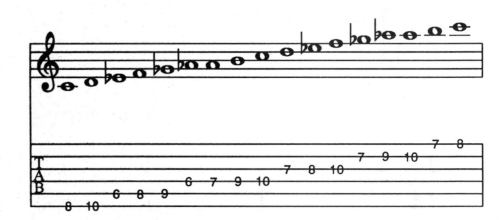

DIMINISHED SCALES

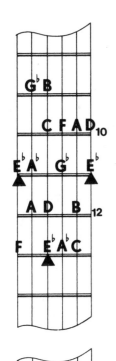

E♭ DIMINISHED SCALE

1		2	3		4	5		6	7		8	9
E♭		F	G♭		A♭	A		B	C		D	E♭

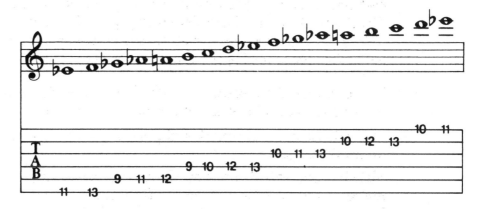

G♭ DIMINISHED SCALE

1		2	3		4	5		6	7		8	9
G♭		A♭	A		B	C		D	E♭		F	G♭

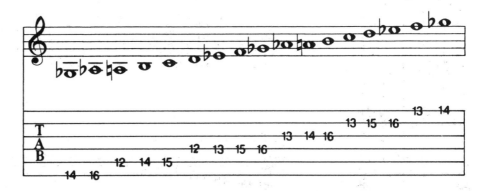

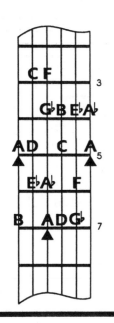

A DIMINISHED SCALE

1		2	3		4	5		6	7		8	9
A		B	C		D	E♭		F	G♭		A♭	A

121

ALTERED SCALES

DISSONANT SCALES

The Enigmatic, Neapolitan and Hungarian Minor scales represent melodic alternatives to traditional diatonic harmonies. While they have a single key-center and may be transposed to all twelve keys, even the most experienced guitarists find them difficult to use, because of their "dissonant" tonal characteristics.

ENIGMATIC SCALE

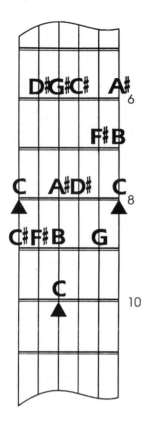

1	2	3	4	5	6	7	8
C	C#	D#	F#	G#	A#	B	C

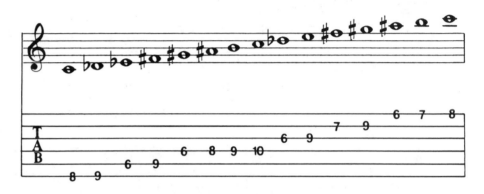

THE ENIGMATIC SCALE. The Enigmatic scale differs from the diatonic major scale in its unusual step, half-step pattern. It has a lowered 2nd, raised 4th, 5th and 6th.

NEOPOLITAN SCALE

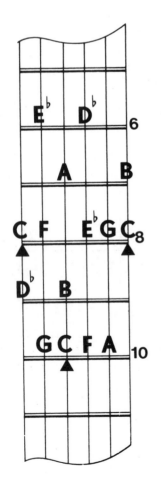

1	2	3	4	5	6	7	8
C	Db	Eb	F	G	A	B	C

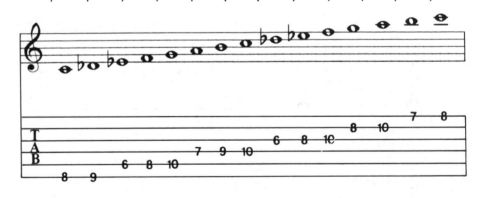

THE NEAPOLITAN SCALE. The Neapolitan scale has a lowered 2nd and 3rd, creating five whole-steps in the middle of the scale.

OTHER SCALES

NEAPOLITAN MINOR SCALE

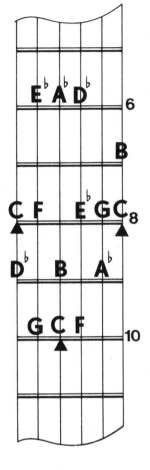

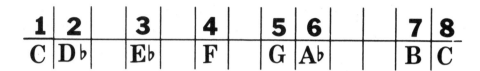

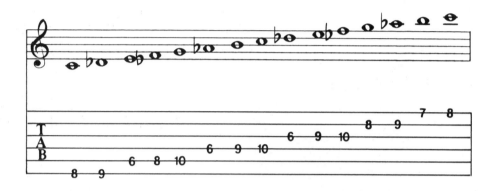

THE NEAPOLITAN MINOR SCALE. The Neapolitan minor scale differs from the diatonic major scale in its lowered 2nd, 3rd and 6th degrees.

HUNGARIAN MINOR SCALE

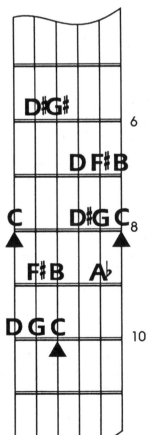

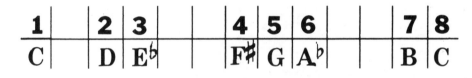

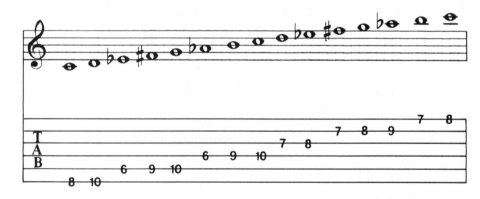

THE HUNGARIAN MINOR SCALE. The Hungarian minor scale differs from the diatonic major scale in its lowered 3rd and 6th, and the raised 4th degrees.

SCALE CHARTS/NOTATION

SCALE CHARTS
SCALE CHARTS
SCALE CHARTS
SCALE CHARTS
SCALE CHARTS
SCALE CHARTS
SCALE CHARTS
SCALE CHARTS
SCALE CHARTS
SCALE CHARTS
SCALE CHARTS
SCALE CHARTS
SCALE CHARTS
SCALE CHARTS
SCALE CHARTS
SCALE CHARTS
SCALE CHARTS
SCALE CHARTS
SCALE CHARTS
SCALE CHARTS

SCALES IN NOTATION
Sight Reading Studies

MAJOR SCALES

Major Diatonic Scale

1		2		3	4		5		6		7	8
C		D		E	F		G		A		B	C
$C^{\sharp}$		$D^{\sharp}$		$E^{\sharp}$	$F^{\sharp}$		$G^{\sharp}$		$A^{\sharp}$		$B^{\sharp}$	$C^{\sharp}$
D		E		$F^{\sharp}$	G		A		B		$C^{\sharp}$	D
$E^{\flat}$		F		G	$A^{\flat}$		$B^{\flat}$		C		D	$E^{\flat}$
E		$F^{\sharp}$		$G^{\sharp}$	A		B		$C^{\sharp}$		$D^{\sharp}$	E
F		G		A	$B^{\flat}$		C		D		E	F
$F^{\sharp}$		$G^{\sharp}$		$A^{\sharp}$	B		$C^{\sharp}$		$D^{\sharp}$		$E^{\sharp}$	$F^{\sharp}$
G		A		B	C		D		E		$F^{\sharp}$	G
$A^{\flat}$		$B^{\flat}$		C	$D^{\flat}$		$E^{\flat}$		F		G	$A^{\flat}$
A		B		$C^{\sharp}$	D		E		$F^{\sharp}$		$G^{\sharp}$	A
$B^{\flat}$		C		D	$E^{\flat}$		F		G		A	$B^{\flat}$
B		$C^{\sharp}$		$D^{\sharp}$	E		$F^{\sharp}$		$G^{\sharp}$		$A^{\sharp}$	B

Fingering Patterns

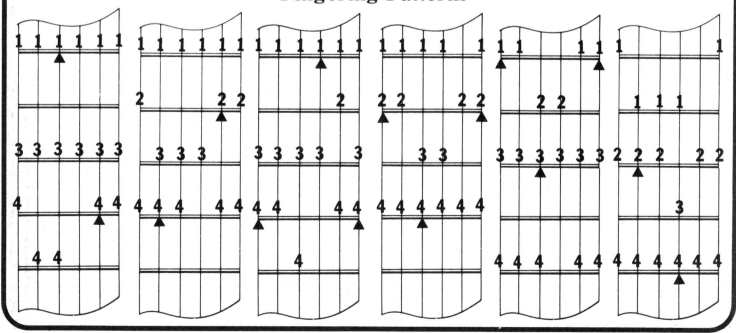

127

SCALES IN NOTATION
Sight Reading Studies

NATURAL MINOR SCALES

NATURAL MINOR SCALES
(Step, Half-Step Pattern)

Aeolian Mode

1	2	3	4	5	6	7	8
C	D	E♭	F	G	A♭	B♭	C
C♯	D♯	E	F♯	G♯	A	B	C♯
D	E	F	G	A	B♭	C	D
D♯	F	F♯	G♯	A♯	B	C♯	D♯
E	F♯	G	A	B	C	D	E
F	G	A♭	B♭	C	D♭	E♭	F
F♯	G♯	A	B	C♯	D	E	F♯
G	A	B♭	C	D	E♭	F	G
G♯	A♯	B	C♯	D♯	E	E♯	G♯
A	B	C	D	E	F	G	A
A♯	B♯	C♯	D♯	E♯	F♯	G♯	A♯
B	C♯	D	E	F♯	G	A	B

Fingering Patterns

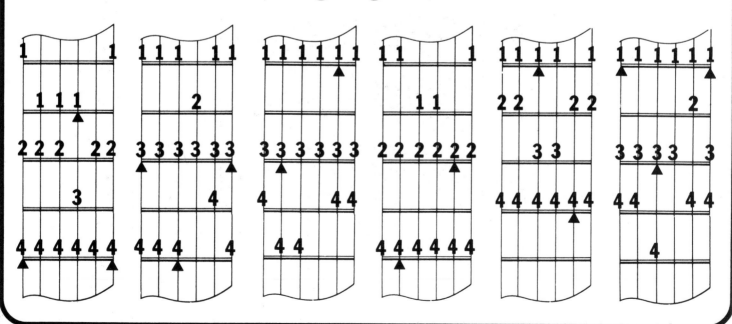

SCALES IN NOTATION

Sight Reading Studies

HARMONIC MINOR SCALES

Harmonic Minor Scale

1		2	3		4		5	6			7	8
C		D	E♭		F		G	A♭			B	C
C♯		D♯	E		F♯		G♯	A			C	C♯
D		E	F		G		A	B♭			C♯	D
D♯		E♯	F♯		G♯		A♯	B			D	D♯
E		F♯	G		A		B	C			D♯	E
F		G	A♭		B♭		C	D♭			E	F
F♯		G♯	A		B		C♯	D			F	F♯
G		A	B♭		C		D	E♭			F♯	G
G♯		A♯	B		C♯		D♯	E			G	G♯
A		B	C		D		E	F			G♯	A
A♯		B♯	C♯		D♯		E♯	F♯			A	A♯
B		C♯	D		E		F♯	G			B♭	B

Fingering Patterns

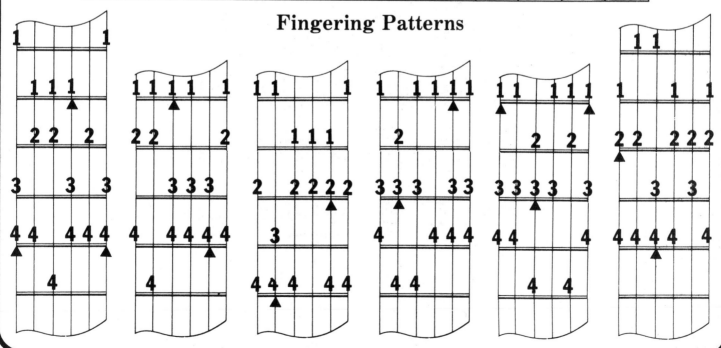

131

SCALES IN NOTATION

Sight Reading Studies

MELODIC MINOR SCALES

Melodic Minor Scale

1		2	3		4	5		6		7	8
C		D	$E\flat$		F	G		A		B	C
$C^\sharp$		$D^\sharp$	E		$F^\sharp$	$G^\sharp$		$B\flat$		C	$C^\sharp$
D		E	F		G	A		B		$C^\sharp$	D
$D^\sharp$		F	$G\flat$		$G^\sharp$	$B\flat$		C		D	$D^\sharp$
E		$F^\sharp$	G		A	B		$C^\sharp$		$D^\sharp$	E
F		G	$A\flat$		$B\flat$	C		D		E	F
$F^\sharp$		$G^\sharp$	A		B	$C^\sharp$		$D^\sharp$		F	$F^\sharp$
G		A	$B\flat$		C	D		E		$F^\sharp$	G
$G^\sharp$		$B\flat$	B		$C^\sharp$	$D^\sharp$		F		G	$G^\sharp$
A		B	C		D	E		$F^\sharp$		$G^\sharp$	A
$B\flat$		C	$D\flat$		$E\flat$	F		G		A	$B\flat$
B		$C^\sharp$	D		E	$F^\sharp$		$G^\sharp$		$B\flat$	B

Fingering Patterns

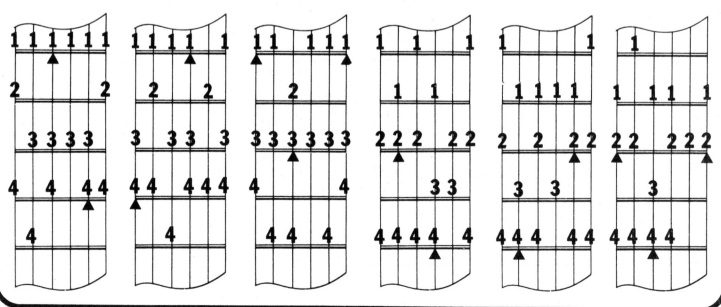

133

SCALES IN NOTATION
Sight Reading Studies

DORIAN MODES

Dorian Mode

1		2	3		4		5		6	7		8
C		D	$E^\flat$		F		G		A	$B^\flat$		C
$C^\sharp$		$D^\sharp$	E		$F^\sharp$		$G^\sharp$		$A^\sharp$	B		$C^\sharp$
D		E	F		G		A		B	C		D
$D^\sharp$		$E^\sharp$	$F^\sharp$		$G^\sharp$		$A^\sharp$		$B^\sharp$	$C^\sharp$		$D^\sharp$
E		$F^\sharp$	G		A		B		$C^\sharp$	D		E
F		G	$A^\flat$		$B^\flat$		C		D	$E^\flat$		F
$F^\sharp$		$G^\sharp$	A		B		$C^\sharp$		$D^\sharp$	E		$F^\sharp$
G		A	$B^\flat$		C		D		E	F		G
$G^\sharp$		$A^\sharp$	B		$C^\sharp$		$D^\sharp$		$E^\sharp$	$F^\sharp$		$G^\sharp$
A		B	C		D		E		$F^\sharp$	G		A
$B^\flat$		C	$D^\flat$		$E^\flat$		F		G	$A^\flat$		$B^\flat$
B		$C^\sharp$	D		E		$F^\sharp$		$G^\sharp$	A		B

Fingering Patterns

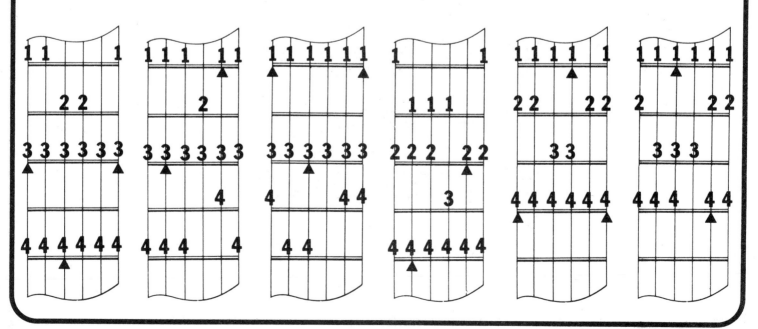

SCALES IN NOTATION
Sight Reading Studies

LYDIAN MODES

Lydian Mode

1		2		3		4	5		6		7	8
C		D		E		F$^\sharp$	G		A		B	C
C$^\sharp$		D$^\sharp$		F		G	G$^\sharp$		A$^\sharp$		C	C$^\sharp$
D		E		F$^\sharp$		G$^\sharp$	A		B		C$^\sharp$	D
D$^\sharp$		F		G		A	A$^\sharp$		C		D	D$^\sharp$
E		F$^\sharp$		G$^\sharp$		A$^\sharp$	B		C$^\sharp$		D$^\sharp$	E
F		G		A		B	C		D		E	F
F$^\sharp$		G$^\sharp$		A$^\sharp$		B$^\sharp$	C$^\sharp$		D$^\sharp$		F	F$^\sharp$
G		A		B		C$^\sharp$	D		E		F$^\sharp$	G
A$^\flat$		B$^\flat$		C		D	E$^\flat$		F		G	A$^\flat$
A		B		C$^\sharp$		D$^\sharp$	E		F$^\sharp$		G$^\sharp$	A
B$^\flat$		C		D		E	F		G		A	B$^\flat$
B		C$^\sharp$		D$^\sharp$		E$^\sharp$	F$^\sharp$		G$^\sharp$		A$^\sharp$	B

Fingering Patterns

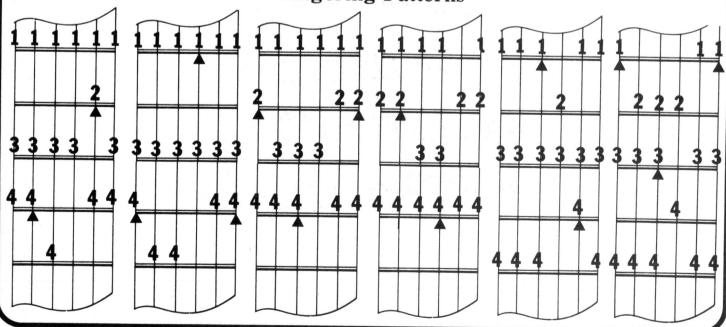

137

SCALES IN NOTATION
Sight Reading Studies

MIXOLYDIAN MODES

Mixolydian Mode

MIXOLYDIAN MODES
(Step, Half-Step Pattern)

1	2	3	4	5	6	7	8
C	D	E	F	G	A	$B^\flat$	C
$C^\sharp$	$D^\sharp$	$E^\sharp$	$F^\sharp$	$G^\sharp$	$A^\sharp$	B	$C^\sharp$
D	E	$F^\sharp$	G	A	B	C	D
$E^\flat$	F	G	$A^\flat$	$B^\flat$	C	$D^\flat$	$E^\flat$
E	$F^\sharp$	$G^\sharp$	A	B	$C^\sharp$	D	E
F	G	A	$B^\flat$	C	D	$E^\flat$	F
$F^\sharp$	$G^\sharp$	$A^\sharp$	B	$C^\sharp$	$D^\sharp$	E	$F^\sharp$
G	A	B	C	D	E	F	G
$A^\flat$	$B^\flat$	C	$D^\flat$	$E^\flat$	F	$G^\flat$	$A^\flat$
A	B	$C^\sharp$	D	E	$F^\sharp$	G	A
$B^\flat$	C	D	$E^\flat$	F	G	$A^\flat$	$B^\flat$
B	$C^\sharp$	$D^\sharp$	E	$F^\sharp$	$G^\sharp$	A	B

Fingering Patterns

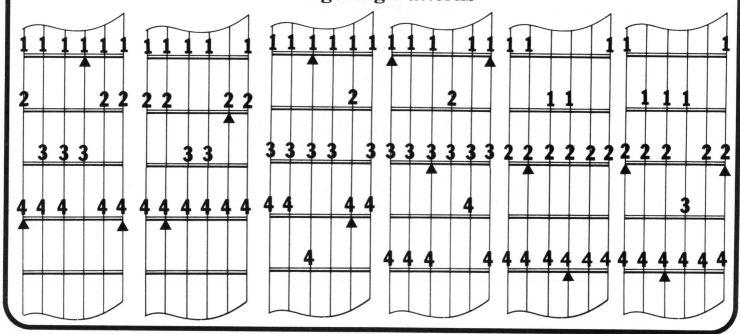

SCALES IN NOTATION
Sight Reading Studies

PHRYGIAN MODES

Phrygian Mode

1	2		3		4		5	6		7		8
C	D♭		E♭		F		G	A♭		B♭		C
C♯	D		E		F♯		G♯	A		B		C♯
D	E♭		F		G		A	B♭		C		D
D♯	E		F♯		G♯		A♯	B		C♯		D♯
E	F		G		A		B	C		D		E
F	G♭		A♭		B♭		C	D♭		E♭		F
F♯	G		A		B		C♯	D		E		F♯
G	A♭		B♭		C		D	E♭		F		G
G♯	A		B		C♯		D♯	E		F♯		G♯
A	B♭		C		D		E	F		G		A
A♯	B		C♯		D♯		E♯	F♯		G♯		A♯
B	C		D		E		F♯	G		A		B

Fingering Patterns

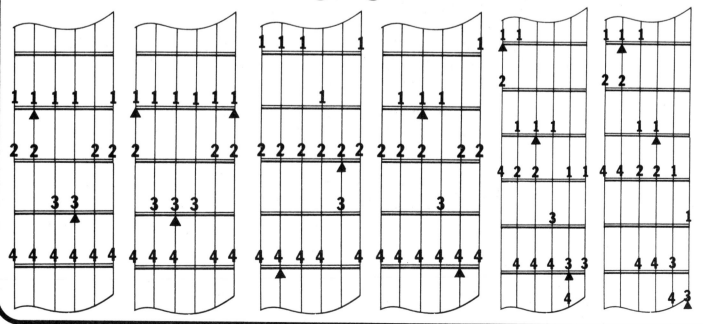

SCALES IN NOTATION
Sight Reading Studies

LOCRIAN MODES

Locrian Mode

1	2		3		4	5		6		7		8
$B^\sharp$	$C^\sharp$		$D^\sharp$		$E^\sharp$	$F^\sharp$		$G^\sharp$		$A^\sharp$		$B^\sharp$
$C^\sharp$	D		E		F	G		A		B		$C^\sharp$
D	$E^\flat$		F		$G^\flat$	$A^\flat$		$B^\flat$		C		D
$D^\sharp$	E		$G^\flat$		$G^\sharp$	A		B		$D^\flat$		$D^\sharp$
E	F		G		A	$B^\flat$		C		$D^\sharp$		E
$E^\sharp$	$F^\sharp$		$G^\sharp$		$A^\sharp$	B		$C^\sharp$		D		F
$F^\sharp$	G		A		B	C		D		E		$F^\sharp$
G	$A^\flat$		$B^\flat$		C	$D^\flat$		$E^\flat$		F		G
$G^\sharp$	A		B		$C^\sharp$	D		E		$F^\sharp$		$G^\sharp$
A	$B^\flat$		C		D	$E^\flat$		F		G		A
$A^\sharp$	B		$C^\sharp$		$D^\sharp$	E		$F^\sharp$		$G^\sharp$		$A^\sharp$
B	C		D		E	F		G		A		B

Fingering Patterns

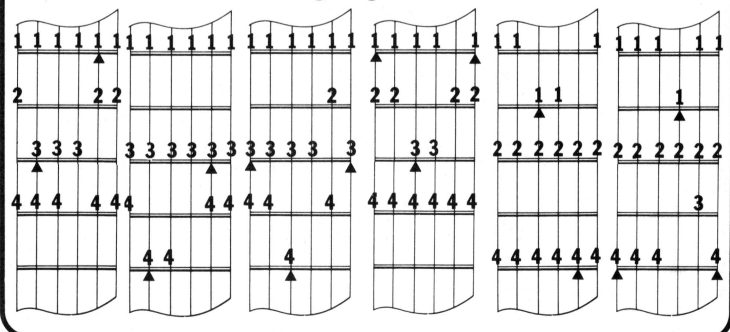

143

SCALES IN NOTATION
Sight Reading Studies

PENTATONIC MAJOR SCALES

Pentatonic "Country" Scale

PENTATONIC MAJOR SCALES
(Step, Half-Step Pattern)

1	2	3	5	6	8
C	D	E	G	A	C
C♯	D♯	F	G♯	A♯	C♯
D	E	F♯	A	B	D
E♭	F	G	B♭	C	E♭
E	F♯	G♯	B	C♯	E
F	G	A	C	D	F
F♯	G♯	A♯	C♯	D♯	F♯
G	A	B	D	E	G
A♭	B♭	C	E♭	F	A♭
A	B	C♯	E	F♯	A
B♭	C	D	F	G	B♭
B	C♯	D♯	F♯	G♯	C

Fingering Patterns

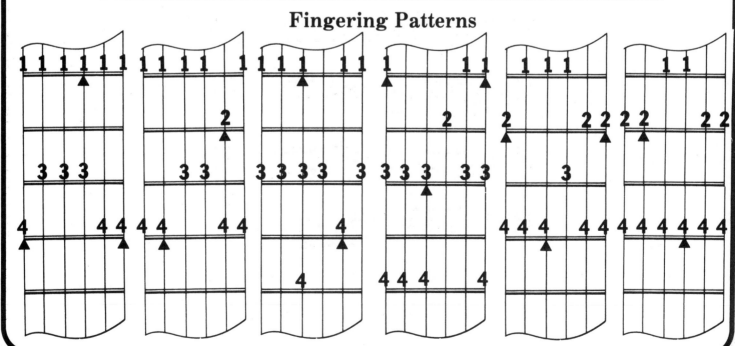

145

SCALES IN NOTATION
Sight Reading Studies

PENTATONIC MINOR SCALES

5-Note "Blues"

1	3	4	5	7	8
C	E♭	F	G	B♭	C
C♯	E	F♯	G♯	B	C♯
D	F	G	A	C	D
E♭	G♭	A♭	B♭	D♭	E♭
E	G	A	B	D	E
F	A♭	B♭	C	E♭	F
F♯	A	B	C♯	E	F♯
G	B♭	C	D	F	G
A♭	B	D♭	E♭	G♭	A♭
A	C	D	E	G	A
B♭	D♭	E♭	F	A♭	B♭
B	D	E	F♯	A	B

Fingering Patterns

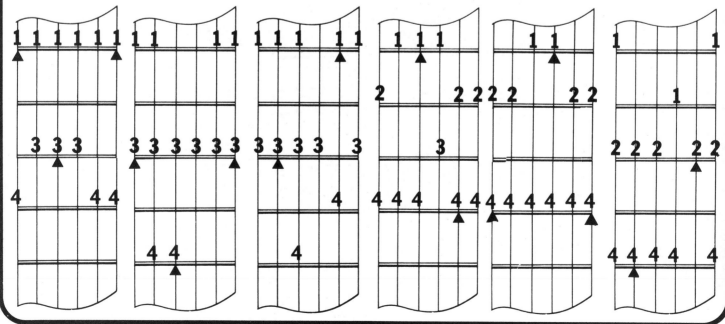

147

SCALES IN NOTATION
Sight Reading Studies

PENTATONIC MINOR SCALES

6-Note "Blues"

PENTATONIC MINOR SCALES
(Step, Half-Step Pattern)

1			3		4	4	5			7		8
C			E♭		F	F♯	G			B♭		C
D♭			E		G♭	G	A♭			B		D♭
D			F		G	G♯	A			C		D
E♭			G♭		A♭	A	B♭			D♭		E♭
E			G		A	A♯	B			D		E
F			A♭		B♭	B	C			E♭		F
G♭			A		B	C	D♭			E		G♭
G			B♭		C	C♯	D			F		G
A♭			B		D♭	D	E♭			G♭		A♭
A			C		D	D♯	E			G		A
B♭			D♭		E♭	E	F			A♭		B♭
B			D		E	F	F♯			A		B

Fingering Patterns

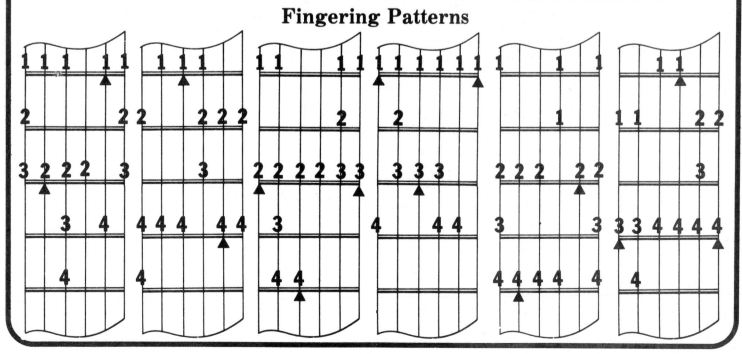

SCALES IN NOTATION
Sight Reading Studies

WHOLE-TONE SCALES

Whole-Tone Scales

1	2	3	4	5	6	8
C	D	E	$F^\sharp$	$G^\sharp$	$A^\sharp$	C
$C^\sharp$	$D^\sharp$	F	G	A	B	$C^\sharp$
D	E	$F^\sharp$	$G^\sharp$	$A^\sharp$	C	D
$E^\flat$	F	G	A	B	$D^\flat$	$E^\flat$
E	$F^\sharp$	$G^\sharp$	$A^\sharp$	C	D	E
F	G	A	B	$C^\sharp$	$D^\sharp$	F
$F^\sharp$	$G^\sharp$	$A^\sharp$	C	D	E	$F^\sharp$
G	A	B	$C^\sharp$	$D^\sharp$	F	G
$A^\flat$	$B^\flat$	C	D	E	$G^\flat$	$A^\flat$
A	B	$C^\sharp$	$D^\sharp$	F	G	A
$B^\flat$	C	D	E	$G^\flat$	$A^\flat$	$B^\flat$
B	$C^\sharp$	$D^\sharp$	F	G	A	B

Fingering Patterns

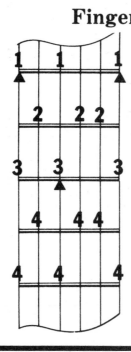
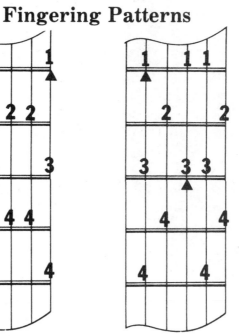
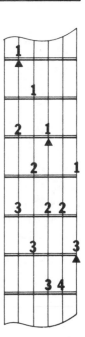

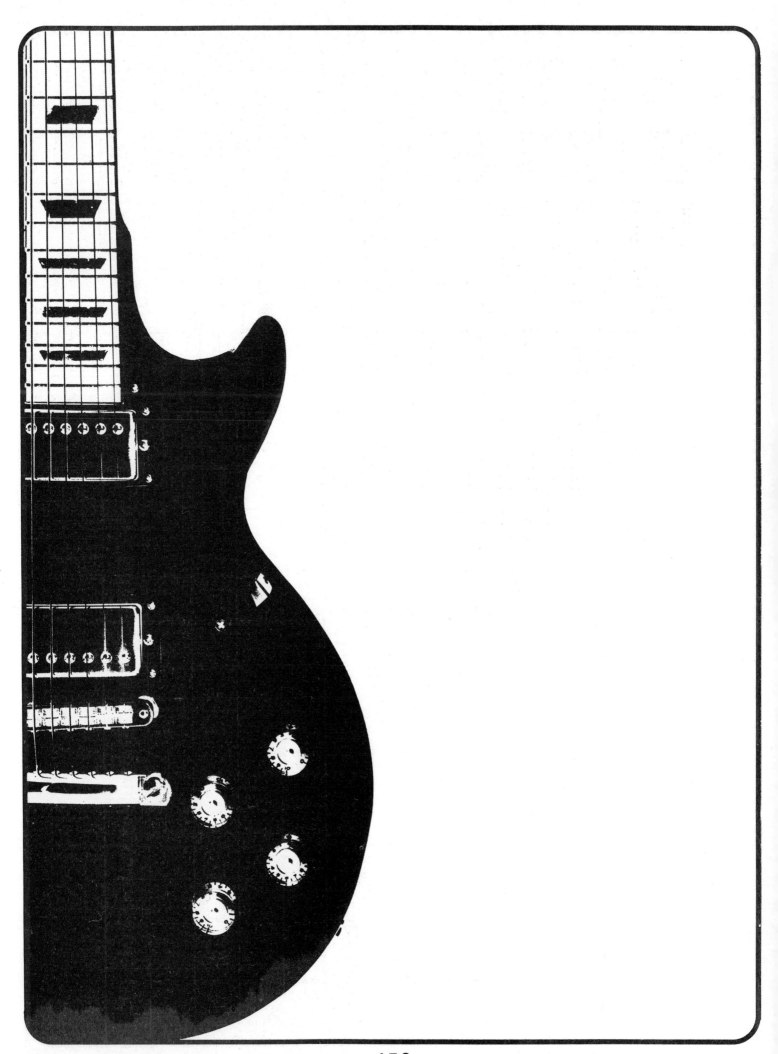

RHYTHM STUDIES
RHYTHM STUDIES
RHYTHM STUDIES
RHYTHM STUDIES
RHYTHM STUDIES
RHYTHM STUDIES
RHYTHM STUDIES
RHYTHM STUDIES
RHYTHM STUDIES
RHYTHM STUDIES
RHYTHM STUDIES
RHYTHM STUDIES
RHYTHM STUDIES
RHYTHM STUDIES
RHYTHM STUDIES
RHYTHM STUDIES
RHYTHM STUDIES
RHYTHM STUDIES
RHYTHM STUDIES
RHYTHM STUDIES
RHYTHM STUDIES

RHYTHM STUDIES

RHYTHM STUDIES

Rhythm Studies is a method of applying the scale concepts presented in this book. At this point, don't get bogged down with the "theory" aspect — now, you should work toward "ear training", and the memorization of scale patterns.

The 5-note patterns can be applied to all scales presented in this book. Should you not be proficient at "alternate picking" and playing "triplets", practice each scale using these techniques.

PRACTICING SCALES

The hands are faster than the eye ... so, watching the hands actually slows you down and causes playing errors. Practice scales with your eyes closed! Practice finger training and ear training. Once familiar with the fingering patterns, try improvising new rhythmic patterns. Skip around within the pattern, train the fingers to move smoothly. There are no short cuts to "good playing" ... all it takes is PRACTICE!

RHYTHM STUDIES

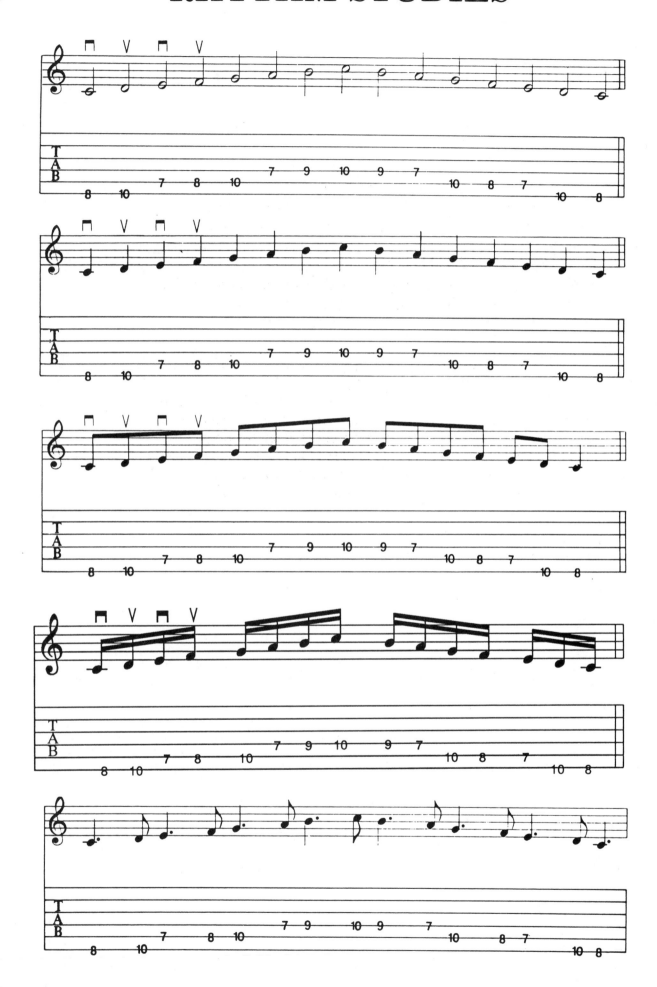

RHYTHM STUDIES

RHYTHM STUDIES

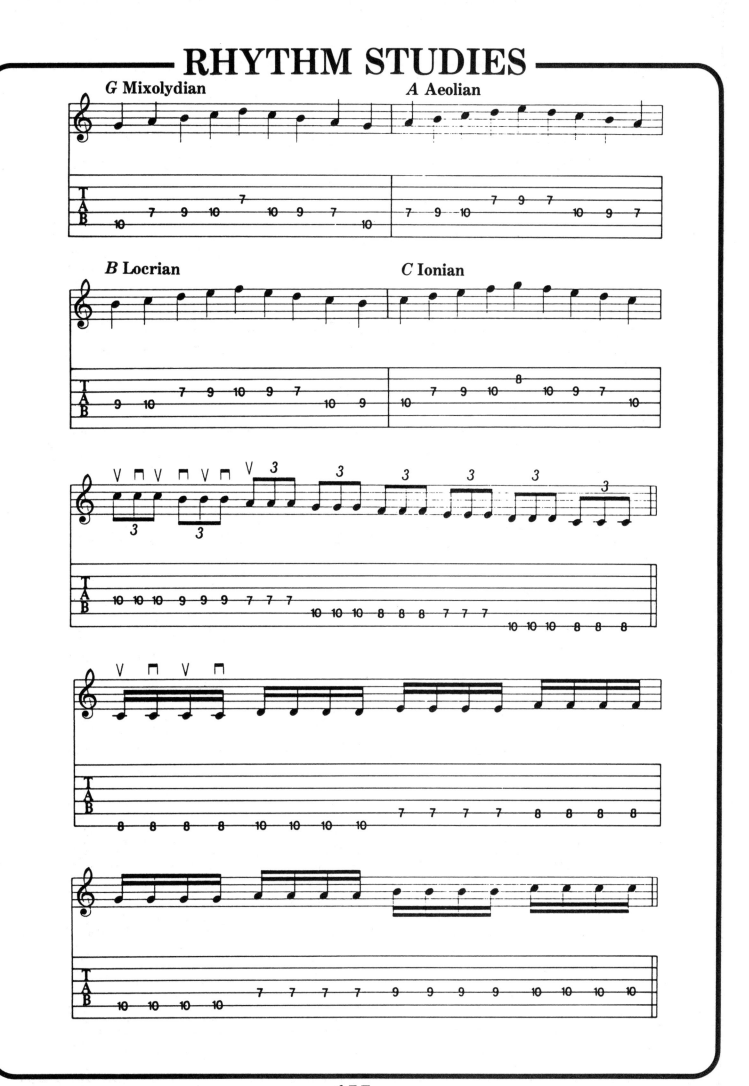